Felt to Stitch

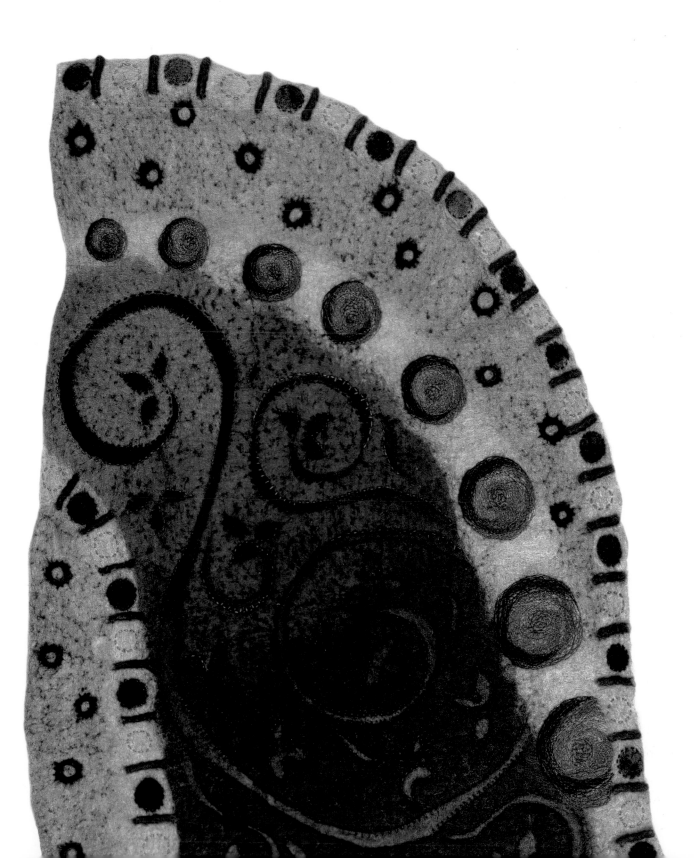

Felt to Stitch

SHEILA SMITH

BATSFORD

ACKNOWLEDGEMENTS

My thanks must go to felt artists Linda Hume, Sarah Lawrence, Jackie Lunn and Jenny Pepper for generously allowing me to include their work in this book.

Thanks also to my students, for asking questions and expecting answers; their curiosity and enthusiasm over the years have encouraged me to experiment and explore new ideas.

Last, but not least, I would like to thank my long-suffering husband for his unstinting interest and support.

First published in the United Kingdom in 2006 by
Batsford
10 Southcombe Street
London
W14 0RA

An imprint of Anova Books Company Ltd

ISBN 9780713490084

A CIP catalogue record for this book is available from the British Library.

15 14 13 12 11 10 09 08 07
10 9 8 7 6 5 4 3

Reproduction by Anorax Imaging Ltd, Leeds, UK
Printed and bound by Craft Print International Ltd, Singapore

This book can be ordered direct from the publisher at the website: www.anovabooks.com, or try your local bookshop.

Distributed in the United States and Canada by Sterling Publishing Co., 387 Park Avenue South, New York, NY 10016, USA

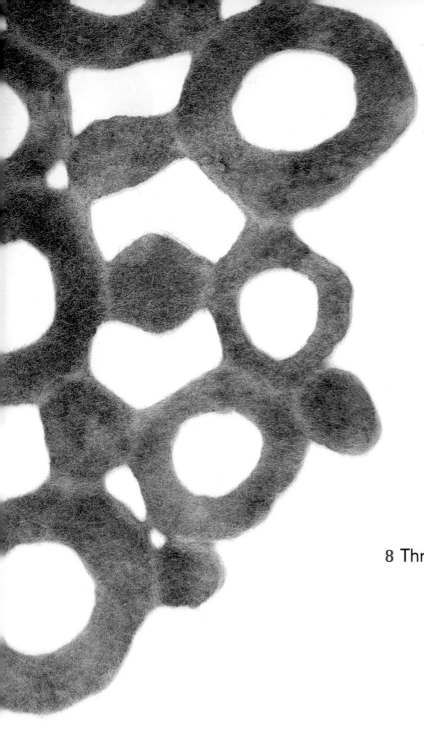

Contents

Introduction

Introduction

Felt is probably one of the oldest known textiles, with a history dating back to around 600 BC. To the nomadic peoples of Central Asia, it was an essential part of their daily lives. It was used as the outer covering for the wooden-framed tents in which they lived and also as carpets to furnish and decorate the tents. Felt is still being made today in countries such as Kyrgyzstan and Kazakhstan. More recently, the interest in felt has increased as textile enthusiasts have discovered the possibilities of felt as a textile medium. After all this time, the basic principles of feltmaking remain unchanged – the essential ingredient is wool, which becomes felt with the addition of moisture, friction and some heat. Contemporary feltmakers combine these essentials in different ways to achieve a diverse range of results.

This book is intended for anyone with an interest in felt. It is aimed at embroiderers and quilters, to encourage them to experiment with methods of creating felted fabrics. It is also intended for feltmakers, in the hope that they will find new techniques with which to extend their practice. It is a book about techniques of preparing felt as a base for stitching rather than completed works, but a small number of projects are included to suggest some initial answers to the question: 'Where to go now?'

Although this is not intended as a technical manual, but rather an ideas book, it is essential for beginner feltmakers to understand the process to enable them to have control over the results.

WHAT HAPPENS WHEN WOOL FELTS

Each individual wool fibre is covered with a layer of overlapping scales. When wool gets wet, it becomes elastic and the scales open up. If friction is added to a bundle of wet wool fibres, the scales become displaced and entangled with each other. The more friction that is applied, the greater the entanglement. At the same time, the fibres begin to shrink and the result is felt. This is an irreversible process, as anyone who has accidentally felted a wool sweater by washing it too vigorously will be aware.

CHOICE OF WOOL

Wool is available from a wide variety of breeds and in a wide range of qualities. While all wools will felt to some degree, some will felt more quickly than others. Fibre thickness is an important factor in the quality of wool and is usually classified in the United Kingdom by the Bradford Count system, while in other parts of the world fibre thickness is measured in microns. The Bradford Count predates the industrial revolution and is based on the number of skeins of wool, each 560 yards in length,

Previous spread: The Blues. This piece combines a range of techniques including colour blending of fibres, inclusion of fabric pieces and simple stitches added at different stages of the felting process.

that could be spun from a one-pound weight of wool. The higher the number, the finer the wool. A micron is a measurement of fibre width: one micron is equal to one millionth of a metre.

System	Coarse	Medium	Fine
Bradford Count	40/44s	56s	64s
Microns	37	28	22
Breed example	Swaledale	Blue-faced Leicester	Merino

COMMERCIAL PREPARATION OF WOOL

The first stage in the commercial preparation of wool is scouring or washing to remove dirt, vegetation, natural grease and sweat. Wool is then dried and carded by machinery with revolving drums coated with small wires to open up the wool and deliver it as a continuous web of fibre, known as a carded batt. Long strips, known as carded sliver, are divided from the batt into long, loose ropes ready for spinning. In both of these forms, the fibres lie in different directions. Another method of preparation, used for finer wools, takes the processing further by removing all short fibres and then combing and stretching the remaining fibres into long, loose ropes with all the fibres lying in a vertical position. The resulting ropes are known as wool tops. Most wool sold for feltmaking is sold in the form of combed tops.

Right: *Traditional Kyrgyz inlaid mosaic design.*

Making Hand-Rolled Felt

1 Making Hand-Rolled Felt

CHOICE OF FIBRE

The quality of a felt relates directly to the choice of fibre, the nature of the fibre depending on the breed of sheep from which the wool is taken. Fine lightweight felt can only be made from fine fibre, while hardwearing firm felt requires a coarser fibre. Below are some examples:

- *Merino* is a soft, fine fibre, suitable for garments and lightweight felt that will drape.
- *Shetland* is also soft and fine and is available in a range of natural colours.
- *Blue-faced Leicester* is a stronger fibre than merino and Shetland, but felts well. It is suitable for outdoor clothing and soft-furnishing fabrics.
- *Wensleydale*, a long-stapled, lustrous fibre with curly locks, is often dyed and used as decoration, but the fleece felts well and produces a strong serviceable felt.
- *Swaledale, Herdwick* and *Black Welsh Mountain* are all hill and mountain sheep, producing wool that is strong, sometimes with coarse fibres. The wool is slower to felt than that of the finer breeds, but produces strong, hardwearing felt, suitable for slippers, bags and rugs.

Further information on different breeds of sheep, and their wools, can be obtained from the British Wool Marketing Board (see page 126 for more information).

FELTMAKING EQUIPMENT

Equipment for feltmaking is simple, inexpensive and easy to improvize.

What you will need

Old towels
Bamboo/matchstick mat
Bubble wrap (with small bubbles)
Length of heavy wooden dowelling or broom handle
Net curtain fabric
Plastic bottle with small holes drilled in the lid
Waterproof apron
Rubber gloves
Plastic carrier bag – lightweight supermarket type

Previous spread: detail of Kyrgyz shirdak mosaic felt. The stitching is there both for decoration and to increase the strength of the felt.

Above: Some feltmaking
equipment − bamboo mat,
wooden dowel, bubble wrap,
sprinkler bottle, hand carders,
net curtain.

Thick string
Soap jelly (see recipe on page 14)
Wool tops

- Old towels are used as a base to work on and to absorb any excess water.
- Bamboo mats provide a textured surface on which to make felt. They are sold as window blinds and can be obtained in various widths from home furnishing departments or DIY stores. The mat needs to be larger than the felt to be made (remove the blind fittings before using). If this type of mat is not available, a lighter weight of reed mat, of the type intended for use as a beach mat, may be substituted. A good width for general purposes is 75cm−1 metre (30−40 in).
- Bubble wrap is placed on the bamboo mat in the early stages of the felting process. Wool fibres are laid on the plastic so that when the fibres are wetted the plastic prevents the water from draining away. Choose the type sold as packaging material, which has small bubbles.

- The length of broom handle/wooden dowelling should be approximately 2–4cm (¾–1.5in) in diameter and as long as the bamboo mat is wide. The dowel provides a rigid centre when rolling the fibres in the bamboo mat.
- The piece of net should be larger than the felt to be made. Lightweight synthetic curtain net is ideal; alternatively, you can use fly-screen netting. Whichever net you choose, it is important that the mesh should be fairly open.
- The plastic bottle is used to sprinkle soap solution over the wool fibres. It should have fine holes bored in the lid and should have a capacity of 1 litre (1¾ pint).
- A plastic carrier bag, folded into a pad, is used to press the water into the wool.
- Thick string is needed to tie up the felt roll.
- An apron and rubber gloves are required for protection.

PREPARING SOAP JELLY
What you will need
Plastic measuring jug
Soap flakes
Kettle/jug, for boiling water
Spoon (dessert size)
Small whisk
Several small plastic jars with lids
Plastic sprinkler bottle (1 litre [1¾ pint] capacity)

Method
1 Half-fill the plastic measuring jug with soap flakes.
2 Pour boiling water into the jug until it is full.
3 Whisk the mixture until the soap flakes dissolve.
4 Pour the soap solution into the small jars and allow it to cool, uncovered. When the solution is cold and solidified the lids can be screwed into place. Use as required.

Using soap jelly to make felting solution
Soap jelly is used to make felting solution for feltmaking.

1 Measure 1 dessert spoon of soap jelly into the plastic measuring jug.
2 Pour 200ml boiling water in to the jug and whisk until the soap is dissolved.
3 Pour this mixture into the sprinkler bottle and top up to 1 litre (1¾ pint) with cold water. Screw the cap tightly into position.

MAKING FELT

Preparing the work area

1   Lay the towel out on a flat surface.
2   Place the bamboo mat on the towel.
3   Lay bubble wrap on the towel, bubble side up.
4   Make up 1 litre (1¾ pint) of felting solution.
5   Collect all the equipment together.

Method

1   Pull out small tufts, 8–10cm (3¼–4in) in length, of wool tops and place them in a line on the bubble wrap, along one side of the mat.
2   Lay out a second line of fibre tufts, half overlapping the first line (like tiles on a roof). Continue in this way until the required area has been covered.
3   Place a second layer of fibres on top of the first layer and at right angles to it (see diagram).
4   Place a third layer of fibres in position. This top layer may be placed at random and in whatever direction you wish in order to achieve the effect for the pattern required. (When preparing a series of samples it is useful to try a variety of methods on the top layer in order to see the different possible effects.)

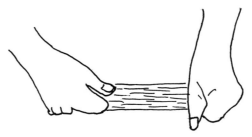

1. Pulling out tufts of wool from wool tops

Right: Laying out fibres for
making a sheet of felt.

2. First layer of fibres

3. Second layer, placed at right angles to the first

5   Cover the fibres carefully with net.

6   Sprinkle felting solution over the net-covered fibres, adding just enough to wet the fibres.

7   Using a large lightweight plastic bag, made into a pad which is larger than your hand, gently press down on the fibres to push the water down through the layers of wool. Next, rub in a circular motion, working from the centre outwards until the fibres are wet through and there are no pockets of air between them. The fibres should lie flat; if necessary, add more water to achieve this.

8   Remove the net gently.

9   Place the broom handle on the edge of felt that is nearest to you and roll the bubble wrap and the wool firmly around the broom handle. Tie each end with thick string to keep the roll tight.

10 Roll it backwards and forwards on the work surface 100 times, pressing firmly down on the roll. Open up the roll and stretch out the felt to ensure that there are no creases; give it a quarter turn, and roll again 100 times.

11 After the second rolling, carefully lift the felt from the bubble wrap and place it on the bamboo mat, quarter turning as before.

12 Roll the felt tightly in the bamboo mat and roll 100 times. Unroll; turn felt again and roll another 100 times.

13 Test the piece to see if the fibres are felted. To do this, try to pick up a few fibres between finger and thumb; if felting is complete, they will not lift from the surface. A second method of testing is to take hold of one corner of the felt and move it between thumb and fingers; there should be no movement between the layers of fibres.

14 If the required degree of felting has not been reached, continue rolling the fibres in the mat, this time without the wooden roller. Roll 50 times in each direction.

THINGS TO LOOK OUT FOR

- During felting, the fibres will shrink in the direction of rolling, so it is important to check the size after each rolling and also to change the direction of rolling each time. In this way, the feltmaker can control the final shape of the piece.

- The degree of felting required is dependent on the desired end result. Functional pieces need to be hardwearing and therefore require more felting. A decorative piece may be left softer – the choice is up to the feltmaker.

- Remember to allow for shrinkage when planning a project. Different wools shrink at different rates, so it is best to sample each type of wool before embarking on a major project. An average allowance for shrinkage is approximately one third.

Right: Laying out fibres for
making a sheet of felt (cont).

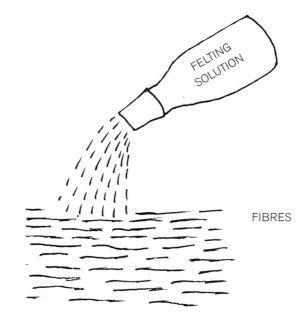

4. Sprinkle felting
solution over fibres

FIBRES

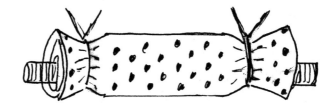

5. Press solution through
fibres with a plastic bag

6. Rolled around
broom handle in
bubble wrap

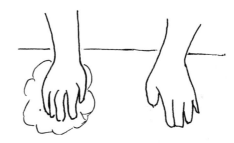

7. Rolling in
bamboo mat

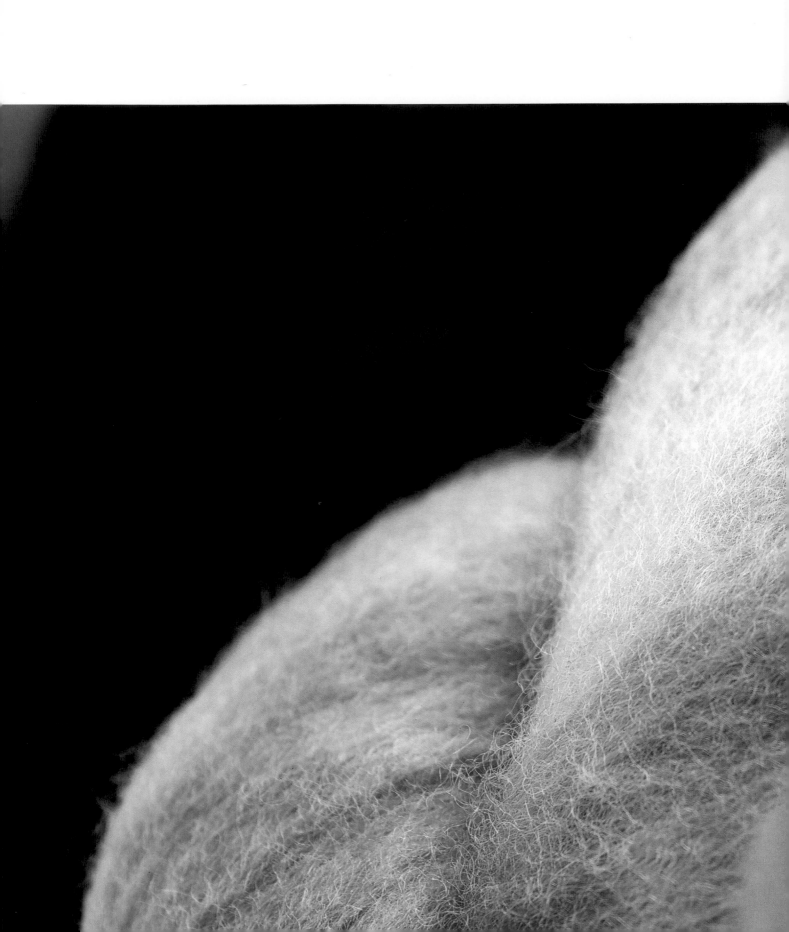

Colour in Felt 2

2 Colour in Felt

The felting process has an important effect on the final colour of a piece. As already explained in the introduction, each individual wool fibre shrinks, wriggles and becomes entangled with other fibres as it felts. If the fibres are of different colours, they will affect each other as they felt together, somewhat as paints do when mixed or blended. This happens when colours are randomly placed in a layer, but also when layers of different colours are placed one on top of another, so thought must be given to the placement of colours.

Just as the choice and positioning of colours affects the final result, so does the method used to apply the colours. Feltmaking is sometimes referred to as 'painting with wool' and some of the principles of painting can be applied to felt. It can be helpful to study the paintings of well-known artists and observe how they use colour.

- If a gentle blend of colours is required, with one colour moving gradually into another, this can be achieved in the preparation of the fibre by carding the colours before felting (see below).
- Another method of mixing colours at the fibre stage is to chop the dry fibres into small pieces, mix the colours and sprinkle them on to the surface. This gives a different effect, reminiscent of the pointillist technique used by some of the Impressionist painters in the 19th century. The colours stay as individual spots yet appear to merge optically.
- Stronger, linear or swirling effects are created by applying the colour boldly in different directions, to emphasize the movement required.
- A solid area of colour is obtained by overlapping and layering fibres, as in the basic feltmaking instructions.

COLOUR MIXING

By blending wool fibres to achieve the required colour, interesting results can be produced. Each individual wool fibre already has its own colour – a product of the original dyeing – and will retain this even when blended with other fibres. The mixes obtained are constituted from the separate colours and add interest to the felt. Coloured wools can thus be blended to produce different colours, or they can be blended with white to produce tints or black to produce shades.

The simplest but fairly time-consuming method of mixing coloured wools is to pull short lengths from wool tops in the required colours, tease them out by hand, mix the colours, and continue teasing until the required colour is obtained.

Previous spread: Merino tops rainbow-dyed with acid dyes and fixed by steaming.

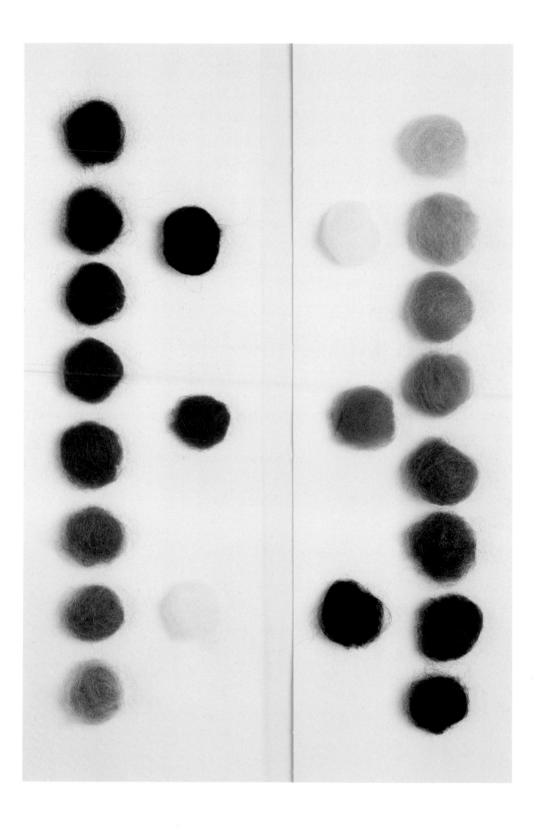

Right: Colour blends from commercially dyed wool tops. Tints and shades are achieved by blending the chosen colour with different proportions of white or black.

Carding

A more efficient method than teasing and mixing is to card the colours together. Carders are wooden tools used by hand spinners to straighten wool prior to spinning. The face of each carder is covered with fine wires, closely set into a sheet of rubbery material, mounted on a wooden base. To use carders for blending coloured wool fibres, the fibres are first hooked on to the left-hand carder in the required proportions and the right-hand carder is then drawn gently down the fibres in a brushing action until the fibres are straight. Next, the fibres are transferred to the right-hand carder and the process is repeated. This is continued until the colours are mixed. Dog-grooming brushes are smaller than carders, but of similar construction, and can be used in the same way.

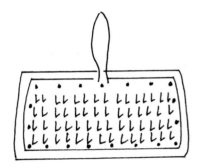

1. Single carder with wire hooks set into leather nailed to wooden base. Used in pairs

2. Pair of carders in use. Tufts of wool hooked on to wires on one carder. The second carder is brushed lightly across the wool

Left: Carding.

Right: Colour swatches from blending primary colours. A range of hues are achieved by blending blue and red in varying proportions.

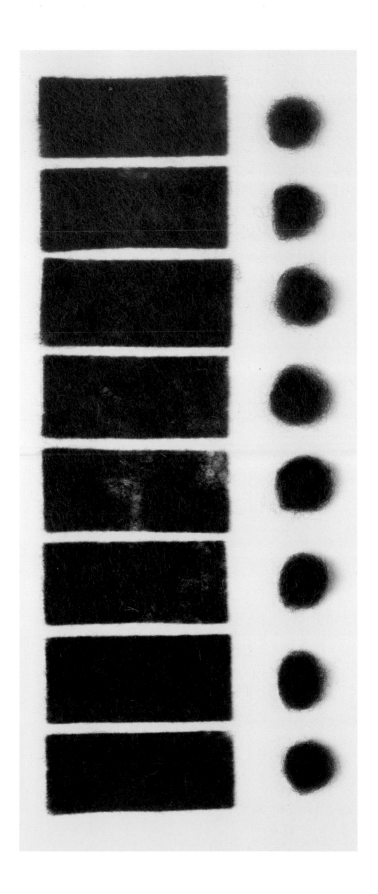

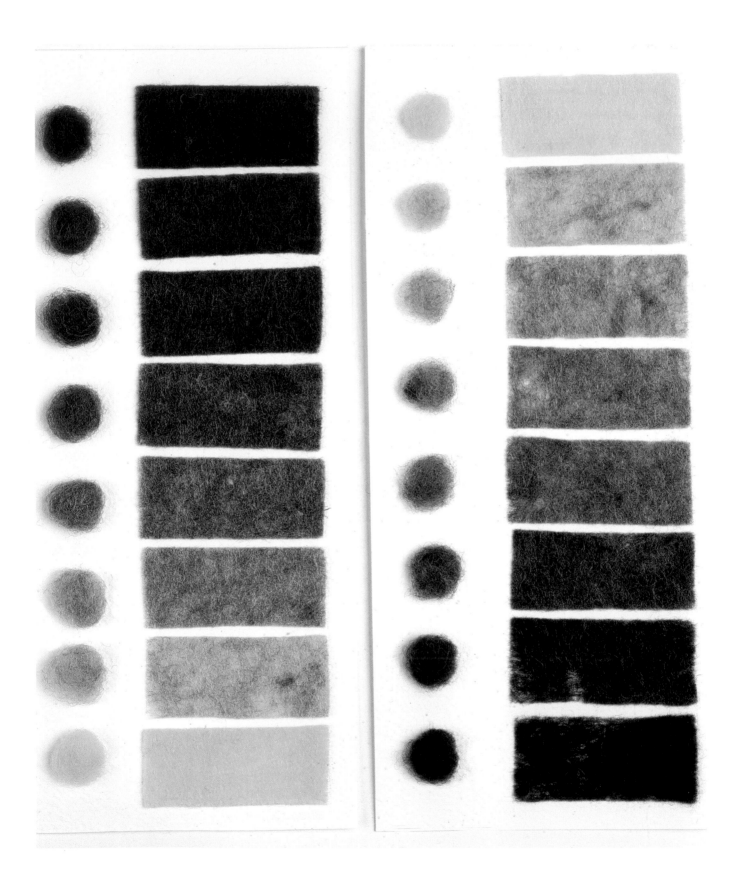

Left: Colour swatches from
blending primary colours:
blue and yellow (left); yellow
and red (right).

Right: Colour swatches from
blending complementary colours,
which produces a range of subtle
colours: purple to yellow (left);
orange to blue (middle); green
to red (right).

Layering colours

Different colours within the layers of felt also affect each other. During the felting process, fibres move within the fibre mass and join with those that lie close to them in the same layer and in the layers above and below. This sample illustrates the effect of laying coloured fibres on white, grey and black and also the effect of different methods of laying out the surface fibres.

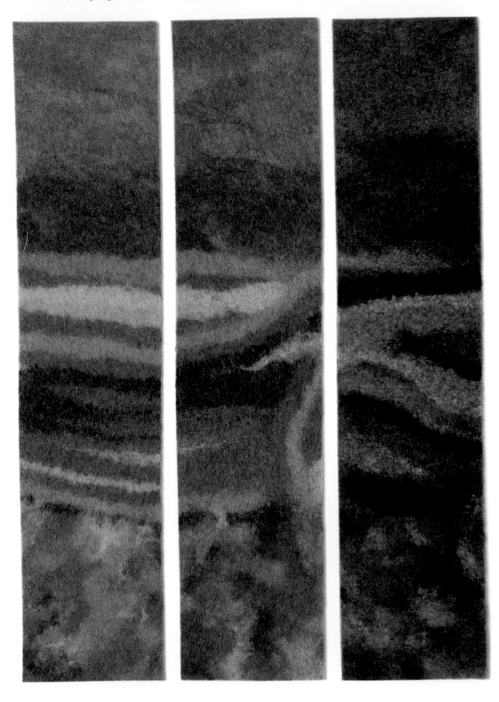

Left: Coloured fibres applied to produce different results within the felt. From top to bottom, fibres were blended, laid in a particular direction and chopped. Coloured fibres were laid on bases of white (left), grey (middle) and black (right).

DYEING WOOL FIBRES

Colour plays an important part in many felt designs. While commercially dyed fibres can be blended to produce the hue or shade required, the feltmaker who understands the basic principles of dyeing wool can produce the range of colours required for each project.

Health and safety when dyeing

The safety aspect is extremely important in all forms of dyeing and great care is required at all times. Some of the chemicals used in dyeing can be harmful if used incorrectly; it is therefore essential to follow these basic safety rules:

1 Always wear rubber gloves and an overall or apron.
2 Protect your work surface with newspaper or polythene sheeting.
3 All utensils should be used exclusively for dyeing. All kitchen equipment should be cleared out of the way before you commence work with dyes.
4 To avoid inhaling dust from dry dye powders, wear a simple protective mask when using the dyes.
5 Avoid inhaling fumes from dye pots – work in a well-ventilated area.
6 All dyestuffs should be stored in sealed containers in a cool dry atmosphere and the contents should be clearly labelled.
7 After dyeing is complete, wash down all work surfaces and carefully wash hands and fingernails.

SIMPLE DYE TECHNIQUES FOR WOOL, USING 'ALL-IN-ONE' ACID DYES

'All-in-one' acid dyes are simple to use, as all the necessary chemicals are combined in the powder. These dyes are intended for use on protein fibres (animal fibres), so are suitable for use on both wool and silk. For this method of dyeing, the dye powder is made up into a solution and applied with a plastic syringe. It is useful to make up the dye solution to a known strength, because this makes it easier to calculate the quantity of dye to apply to the fibres.

What you will need

Scales that will measure weights of 1 gram ($\frac{1}{20}$ oz): diet scales are useful.
Alternatively, you can use a measuring spoon of the type designed for cooking (but remember to keep it only for use with dyes)
Plastic beakers, marked in mililitres (alternatively, use a measuring jug)
Glass rod or similar, for stirring solutions

To make up a 1 per cent dye solution:

1 Weigh 1 gram (1/20 oz) of dye powder and place it in a 100ml (4fl oz) beaker.

2 Add approximately 30ml (just over 1fl oz) of hot water and stir with a glass rod until all the lumps are removed (the process is just like making custard).

3 Carefully fill up the beaker to the 100ml (4fl oz) mark with boiling water, stir thoroughly and allow to cool.

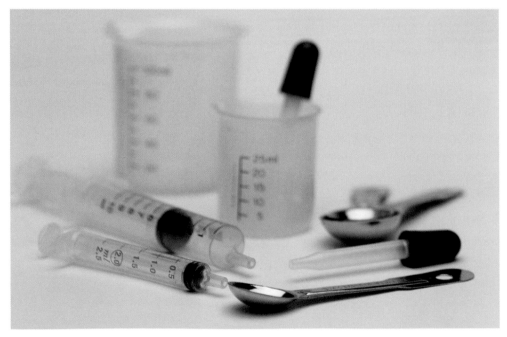

Left: Dyes and equipment – dyes, syringes, beakers, scales and measuring spoons.

DYEING WOOL FOR FELTING

When dyeing wool specifically for making felt, it is important to minimize movement during the process. Heat alone does not cause wool to felt, but heat plus moisture plus friction does. It is therefore essential to keep movement to a minimum. When dealing with small quantities, the use of a steamer will help to prevent excessive movement of the fibres.

What you will need

Bowl for soaking the wool

Liquid detergent

Vinegar

Dye solution

Boil-proof plastic bag and fastener

Electric steamer (alternatively, a metal colander placed over a pan of boiling water may be used)

Note: Remember that when kitchen utensils are used for dyeing, they should be kept only for this purpose and stored separately.

Preparing the wool

Wet the wool thoroughly in warm water, adding a drop of liquid detergent and 50ml (2fl oz) of vinegar to 1 litre (1¾ pint) of water. Leave it to soak for 10 to 15 minutes.

Steaming the wool to set the acid dyes

A simple method of using acid dyes is to steam the wool, as follows:

1 Gently squeeze the excess water from the wool and place it in a boil-proof plastic bag.
2 Add enough dye solution (made up as per instructions for the make of dye to be used) to partially cover the wool.
3 Gently press the wool down into the solution until it has absorbed the dye.
4 Fasten the top of the bag and place it in a steamer.
5 Steam for 30 minutes.
6 Allow the wool to cool. Remove it from the bag and then rinse in lukewarm water until the rinsing water is clear.
7 Squeeze out the excess water and allow the wool to dry.

RAINBOW DYEING

For a more complex effect, the wool can be dyed with more than one colour.

What you will need

Bowl for soaking the wool

Liquid detergent

Vinegar

Large plastic freezer bag

Large plastic tray, such as a cat-litter tray or photographic tray

Dyes

Syringes

Potato masher or rubber gloves

Kitchen foil

Steamer (or colander and pan of boiling water)

Method

1 Prepare the wool as before. Cut open the freezer bag and place in the base of the plastic tray. Squeeze the fibres to remove excess soaking liquid and place them in the tray. They should be wet, but there should be no excess water in the tray.

2 Make up the dye solutions as required and apply with a syringe. Two or more colours may be used.

3 Press the dye gently down into the wool – an old potato masher is useful for this or you can use your hands, if protected with rubber gloves.

4 Turn the fibres over and, if necessary, add more dye solution. The wool should be coloured, but there must be no loose dye solution in the base of the container.

5 Wrap the fibres in the plastic, turning in the ends to avoid spillage. Place the resulting package in a sheet of kitchen foil and seal the ends.

6 Place the foil-wrapped package in the steamer and steam for 40 minutes.

7 Allow the package to cool completely before rinsing the fibres.

8 Gently tease out the fibres to open out the top. Allow the wool to dry.

Microwave dyeing

The processes described above can also be carried out in a microwave, but the wool is more liable to felt if you use this method. Wool that has already been felted can be successfully coloured in a microwave by placing the wetted felt in the base of a microwave container and applying each dye with a syringe. Cover the container with clingfilm and microwave on medium heat for 5 minutes, less for a high-wattage model.

Left: Merino tops rainbow-dyed with acid dyes which are set by steaming.

Line, Shape and Pattern

3 Line, Shape and Pattern

LINE

To interpret a design involving line in felt, it is necessary to study the characteristics of the lines involved. In other words, whether the lines are thick or thin, clear or fuzzy, straight or shaped and so on.

- Lines may be depicted by applying yarns to a base of wool fibres before felting. Different effects will be produced, according to the nature of the yarn used – textured or smooth, thick or thin – so it is important to choose a yarn with characteristics that match your design. It is also important to realize that while you may carefully place yarns on the surface of the wool fibres to interpret a design, they will not remain exactly as you placed them. The felting process will cause the yarns to develop slight but interesting crinkles. This is a characteristic of felt and has to be accepted.
- A second method used to depict lines in felt is to pull thin lengthways strips from the combed tops and lay these on the surface of the felt.
- Use a commercially prepared roving (see page 124).

Previous spread: Turkish Memories (detail). Inlaid design in merino wool with surface machine stitching and beads.

Right: Triangular felt shapes applied to a layer of needle-punched felt, with parallel lines of machine stitching on the surface.

Right: Spun yarns of different thicknesses were applied to the surface of the wool prior to felting. Although the yarns were placed in straight lines, the effect of the movement of the wool fibres during the felting process results in movement of the yarns.

Right: Thick, soft, lightly spun merino wool roving felted into a surface of white merino wool. Running stitches were added after the felting was complete.

GRIDS

Grids are formed by a network of lines running in different directions. The smaller the scale of the grid, the more difficult it is to preserve the clarity of lines in felt. For this reason, it is particularly important that the grid scale and the quality of the line should be balanced.

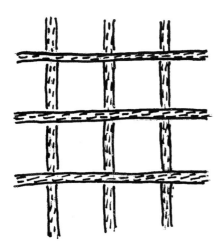

1. Grid of strips of wool tops

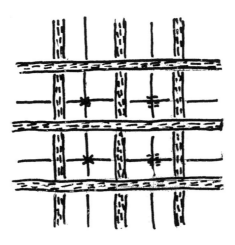

2. Grid of tops interspersed with yarns

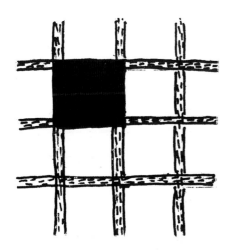

3. Addition of fabric to grid

4. Grid after felting yarns distorted as wool felts

Left: Lines and grids.

To make an open grid of felt, using wool tops

Grid patterns may be formed on a base of wool fibres, using wool tops, or rovings, as follows:

1 Separate pencil-thin strips from the length of top.
2 Lay out strips in the desired pattern on bubble wrap. The spaces between the fibres will enlarge slightly as the wool shrinks, so this needs to be taken into account. A spacing of approximately 5–6cm (2–2½in) is ideal for a first experiment.
3 Carefully cover the grid with net and wet it with felting solution.
4 Remove the net, cover the grid with a second layer of bubble wrap and felt, following the instructions on pages 15–17.
5 As the grid begins to felt, stretch it out in both directions to prevent the lines from distorting.
6 Yarns may be interspersed with strips of wool fibres to add variation to a plain grid, but consider the need to control the crossing points of yarns with the addition of a small amount of wool, or be prepared to stitch these together after felting is completed (see diagram opposite).
7 A further variation is to fill some parts of the grid with fabrics. This is done by cutting pieces of fabric just large enough to fill the chosen space in the grid, plus small turnings around the edges. Place the fabric pieces in position and add a fine line of wool to cover fabric edges – this will ensure a neat and strong edge. Felt as before.
8 During the felting process, the fibres will flatten. If a more rounded effect is required, as the fibres become stronger the lines of the grid may be rolled in the fingers to remove the flat effect.

Above: *Fancy spun synthetic yarns interspersed with the wool grid. As wool shrinks the grid becomes smaller and the yarns hang more loosely because they do not shrink. Each crossing point of the yarns has been controlled by stitching.*

Above: Turkish Memories. Inlaid pre-felted shapes based on traditional Turkish carpet designs.

SHAPE AND PATTERN

To produce patterns or shapes with clearly defined outlines within felt, it is necessary to pre-felt the fibres for the pattern areas before applying the fibre shapes to the background. Pre-felt, as its name suggests, is a sheet of fibres felted just enough to hold them together but not enough to start the shrinking process. Patterns cut from pre-felt retain clear outlines even after felting, as the initial felting discourages the fibres from migrating into the unfelted background fibres.

Making pre-felt

Pre-felt can be made from wool fibres alone, but other fibres, fabrics and thread scraps can be added to the surface to give interest or texture.

Method

1 Place two layers of fibre on bubble wrap (see instructions for making basic felt, page 15).
2 Cover the fibres with net, wet them and then gently flatten them, ensuring that fibres are thoroughly wetted.
3 Remove the net, cover the fibres with a second layer of bubble wrap and roll them up tightly around a wooden dowel. Roll as before (see page 16), turning regularly for a total of around 400 rolls.
4 Remove the fibres from the bubble wrap, place them on to a bamboo mat and roll 50 times along the length and then the width.
5 Test with your fingers to see if the fibres are holding together, but not felting. Rinse the pre-felt and iron with a moderate heat before laying it out flat to dry.

TRADITIONAL TECHNIQUES

Traditional carpet felts are often decorated with clearly defined patterns, which are produced in various ways. In Turkey, traditional designs are cut from the pre-felt and the pattern is first assembled on a large reed mat. Background fibres are then added, covering the pattern to a depth of at least 10cm (4in), after which the whole is wetted, rolled up and felted. These carpets are known as *kece*. Each feltmaking area has its own pattern. In contemporary feltmaking, this technique is usually known as 'inlay'.

Another method is used in central Asia. Here, two differently coloured sheets of fully felted fibres are placed on top of one another. A motif is taken from the centre, the cuts going through both sheets. The two resulting motifs are changed over and set into the felt of the opposite colour, giving a positive/negative effect. The pieces are stitched in position by taking a strong thread over and under the edges (see diagram, right). The seam is then covered with a decorative cord of tightly-twisted woollen thread, which both strengthens and decorates the edge. Finally, the decorated felt is placed on a second backing felt and the two layers are quilted together. This technique is known as *shirdak* in Kyrgyzstan and *syrmak* in Kazakhstan. It could be described as mosaic patchwork.

Both these traditional methods are used extensively in contemporary feltmaking to introduce clear-cut shapes in either a plain or blended background.

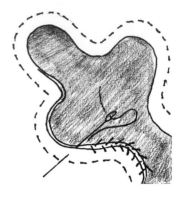

Above: *Diagram of stitching to hold mosaic pieces in place.*

Left: *Felt rug made in Konya, Turkey. Traditional inlaid pattern using pre-felted fibres.*

Right: Shirdak *sample. Mosaic shapes stitched together and seams decorated and strengthened with tightly twisted wool cords. Pattern layer placed on felt backing and tightly quilted together.*

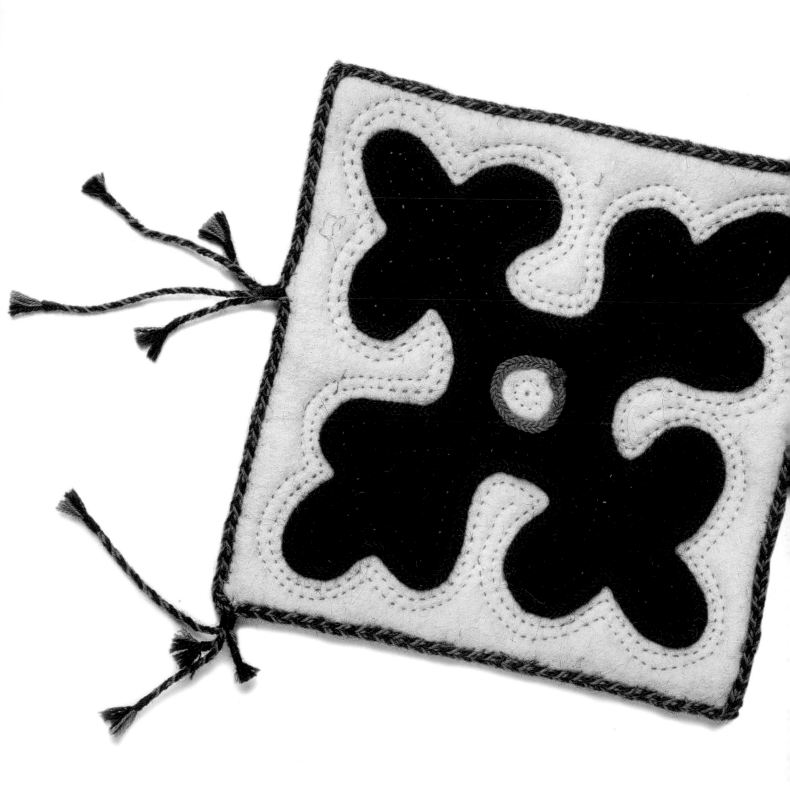

A CONTEMPORARY MOSAIC FELT DESIGN

First consider the type of colour scheme required – whether you are aiming for soft or bright, monochromatic or complementary colours and so on – and then prepare two differently coloured sheets of pre-felt. The resulting felts will be more interesting if the colours are blended. Other fibres, such as silk or flax, and small scraps of fabric or yarns can be added to the surface. Rinse the pre-felts and allow them to dry.

Designing

Prepare a design by drawing or working with paper cutouts to determine the shapes and sizes required.

Preparing the shapes

1 Cut the required shapes in paper to use as templates.
2 Decide which pre-felt is to be the foundation for the design. Position templates on the foundation piece, pin them in position and carefully cut out the shapes.
3 Starting with the largest template, pin it on to the second sheet of pre-felt, carefully selecting an area of colour to harmonize or contrast with the foundation piece.
4 Cut out the shape and transfer this into the matching gap in the foundation piece.
5 Continue in this way until the desired effect is achieved.

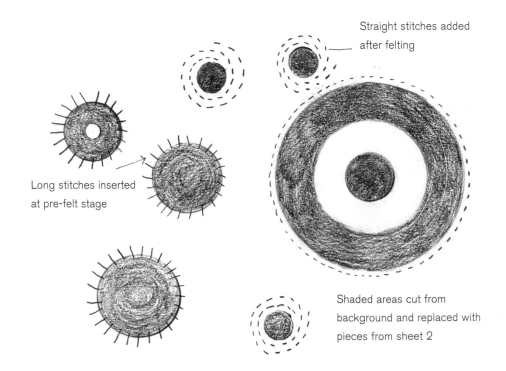

Straight stitches added after felting

Long stitches inserted at pre-felt stage

Shaded areas cut from background and replaced with pieces from sheet 2

Left: Drawings of design for contemporary mosaic

Constructing the mosaic

Once the design is planned and the shapes cut, the inserts can be stitched as invisibly as possible on the wrong side with fine sewing thread in matching colours. Alternatively, a heavier thread and larger stitches can be used on the right side. Further stitches can be added to the surface to add interest at this pre-felted stage.

Completing the felt

1 Lay the reconstructed felt face down on a sheet of bubble wrap.
2 Lay two fine layers of wool tops over the surface.
3 Cover the layers with net and wet the whole package with felting solution.
4 Felt together in the usual way.
5 Rinse, dry and press into shape.
6 Add additional stitching or beads to the surface, if required.

Below: Contemporary mosaic design with surface stitching.

Right: *Print and stitch on merino felt, with stitching added at the pre-felt stage prior to the final felting process to integrate with the felt. Further stitching and printing was added after the felting was complete.*

Other Fibres in Felt

4 Other Fibres in Felt

Silk and cellulose fibres add interesting textures to the surface of felt. These fibres are not themselves able to felt, but the wool fibres attach to them and as the wool shrinks the other fibres are pulled up with them. The fibres may be added in a thin layer to the surface of wool, but if more control is required, they can be made into 'paper' before use.

MAKING QUICK-AND-EASY FIBRE 'PAPER'

This method does not produce a true paper, as it depends on a temporary fixative to hold the fibres in place. The fixative is spray starch, of the type used to stiffen fabric when ironing. This does not make a very robust paper, but it is ideal for use when making felt as it is quick and ready for use immediately.

What you will need

Silicone-treated baking parchment
Silk fibres, such as tops, caps or throwster's waste
Can of spray starch
Iron and ironing board

Method

1 Cut a 1m (40in) length of baking parchment and fold in half.
2 Place it on a flat surface and carefully lay out your chosen fibres, in overlapping rows, on one half of the paper.
3 Spray lightly with starch, taking care not to disturb the fibres.
4 Fold the paper over the fibres and press down.
5 Using a warm iron, press lightly on the parchment paper, pressing first one side then the other.
6 When fibres begin to dry out, gently iron the package on both sides, continuing until the fibres are dry.
7 Uncover the fibres and lift the 'paper' from the parchment.
8 If any fibres are loose, spray them again, where necessary, and iron until dry.

Previous spread: Silk paper in a tile pattern felted on blue-faced Leicester fibre. Silk threads in the silk paper distort as the wool felts and brown wool fibres penetrate the surface of the silk paper, creating an aged effect.

Right: Silk paper with incorporated synthetic nylon fibres.

INCORPORATING THE FIBRE 'PAPER' IN FELT IN A TILE DESIGN

Use folded and cut paper to develop a design, making up a tile pattern (see diagrams below and finished piece opposite). Black paper is good for this, as it shows the design clearly when mounted on white paper.

Method

1 Make fibre paper (see page 48) and cut out motifs (see diagrams below).
2 Lay out three or four fine layers of wool on bubble wrap.
3 Cover the layers with net and wet as usual.
4 Remove the net and place the motifs in position on the wool fibres.
5 Cover the design with a sheet of very thin plastic (the type used for a decorator's dust sheeting is excellent).
6 Press and rub the surface of the plastic gently until the motifs adhere to the surface of the wool.
7 Felt in the usual way, leaving the thin plastic in place to protect the design until the final stages.

When felting is complete, the wool fibres will have penetrated the surface of the paper, giving a slightly crazed or aged look. This can be enhanced by colour choice. The greater the contrast between the colour of the background wool and the fibre paper, the greater the crazed appearance.

BLACK PAPER SQUARE
1. Fold in half diagonally
2. Fold in quarters
3. Cut away white areas
Ensure that part of folded
edges remain uncut

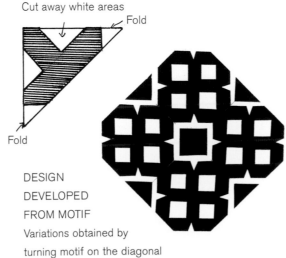

Cut away white areas
Fold
Fold

DESIGN
DEVELOPED
FROM MOTIF
Variations obtained by
turning motif on the diagonal

RESULTING MOTIF (Additional
triangles cut from outside edges)

*Right: Sample swatch: silk fibres and silk
papers in merino felts.*

Above: *Completed silk inlay, using silk paper for the motif.*

A Book Cover

5 A Book Cover

A beautiful handmade cover can turn a sketchbook, journal or photograph album into something special. Felt is the ideal medium, as it does not fray and is easy to handle and manipulate. For a first attempt, choose a book which isn't too small, as felt can be a little thick and clumsy to fit over a very small book. Your book should have hard covers and a spine or wire binding.

Preparation

Measure the book carefully, noting the height and then the width, running from the outer edge of back cover, around the spine and to the outer edge of the front cover. Add 5mm (¼in) to each measurement, to allow for seams. This is the size of the finished felt required.

Next, you need to calculate the area of fibres required, allowing for shrinkage, to make a piece of felt of the required size.

Example:

1 To make finished felt for a cover measuring 50cm (20in) wide by 30cm (12in) high, add one half to each measurement: 50 + 25 = 75cm (30in) and 30 + 15 = 45cm (18in).

2 Lay out fibres to fill an area measuring 75 x 45cm (30 x 18in). One-third shrinkage during felting will reduce these measurements back to 50 x 30cm (20 x 10in).

Note that any of the design methods already described for making decorative flat felt would be suitable for this project.

What you will need

Lightweight iron-on stabilizing fabric, such as Vilene (Pellon)
Fabric for the lining – cotton sateen curtain lining fabric is suitable and comes in a range of colours
Hand-rolled felt

Previous spread: Detail of silk patchwork book cover showing printed silk fabrics included in the felt.

Right: Book cover. Strip patchwork of silk fabrics, stitched together, a fine layer of wool added to the reverse of fabrics and felted, resulting in interesting textures.

Method

1 Cut Vilene (Pellon) to the measurements of the book.

2 Cut lining fabric to the measurements of the book, plus 2.5cm (1in) extra on both width and height.

3 Iron the Vilene (Pellon) in position in the centre of the wrong side of the lining fabric – this will leave 12mm (½in) seam allowances at all edges (see diagram opposite).

4 Cut two flaps from the lining fabric, each measuring approximately 10–12cm (4–4½in) wide by the height measurement of the main lining piece.

5 On each flap, turn a double hem, 12mm (½in) deep, to the wrong side on one of the long edges. Iron the hem in position and machine stitch it in place (see diagram).

6 Place a flap on the short edge of the lining, matching raw edges and with the wrong side of the flap facing the right side of lining. Pin them in position.

7 Trim felt to the correct size (see above), allowing 5mm (¼in) on all edges, for seam allowances.

8 Place lining, with flaps attached, on the wrong side of the felt. Fold in the raw edges of lining so that the fold lies just in from the edge of the felt. Tack (baste) the lining in position. If bookmarks or fastening cords are to be used, they should be inserted between the lining and the felt at this stage.

9 Set the sewing machine stitch to a wide zigzag and medium stitch length and stitch around all the edges to hold the lining in position. Continue building up rows of zigzag stitching on top of each other until a firm edge is achieved. Shaded and metallic threads may be used to create an interesting edge finish. Finally, a few beads may be added as surface decoration.

Left: *Book cover. Inlaid shapes with lurex fabric insertions, stitching at pre-felt stage and additional beads after felting.*

Right: Making your book cover.

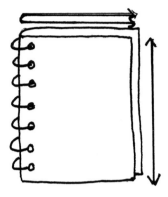

1. Measure height and width all round including spine

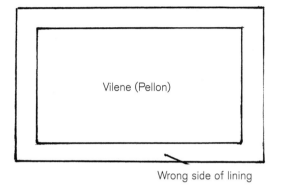

Wrong side of lining

3. Vilene (Pellon) ironed in position

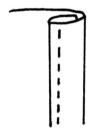

5. Flap hem turned to wrong side

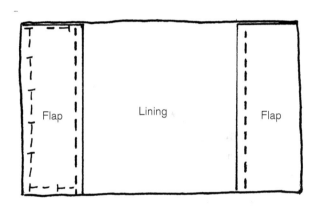

Flap

Lining

Flap

8. Lining placed on the wrong side of the felt

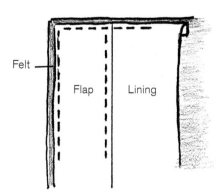

Felt

Flap

Lining

8. Lining tacked (basted) into position

9. Zigzag stitching around the edge

Shibori

6 Shibori

Shibori is a Japanese technique of embellishing textiles by shaping cloth and securing it, usually with knotting and binding, before dyeing. It is used to create patterns on cloth and also to create three-dimensional effects, using combinations of twisting, folding and stitching.

Shibori techniques can be applied to felt at different stages during the felting process – pre-felt or fully felted. If shibori is applied to pre-felt and the felting is then completed with the ties in place, this helps to retain the shaping produced by the ties. If shibori techniques are carried out at the fully felted stage, the aim is more often to produce pattern rather than shape.

Shibori, when used to create pattern, is a resist technique. The cloth is first twisted, folded or pleated, after which tight ties or clamps are applied to compress certain areas. The resulting bundle is then immersed in dye. The ties or clamps prevent the dye from penetrating the compressed areas so that when they are removed patterns have been formed. When dyeing complex patterns, the process can be repeated several times, the fabric being refolded and tied in different areas before being over-dyed in different colours.

As already mentioned, shape can be achieved in felt by binding and tying at the pre-felt stage, before completing the felting process. The shrinkage achieved through felting then locks the shape into the wool. The subsequent felting can be carried out by hand in a bowl of soapy water or in a washing machine. After felting, you should rinse and, if required, dye the felt and then, finally, remove the bindings.

An alternative to pre-felt is needle-punched felt (see page 116), which is similar, but commercially produced. To strengthen either pre-felt or needle-punched felt when tying in objects to produce shape, the wool fibres can be lightly felted to a fabric such as scrim before tying.

The simple shibori technique described below is suitable for use on pre-felt.

1 Tie the pre-felt into a bundle by hand, either with strong thread or with string.
2 Make gathering stitches, either on the flat fabric or over a fold of fabric, and pull them tight.
3 Push small objects, such as marbles, into the felt bundle and bind tightly.

Previous spread: Shibori techniques on merino wool and rainbow-dyed cotton scrim with surface stitching.

STITCHING FOR SHIBORI

Preparation of cotton fabrics for shibori dyeing.

1

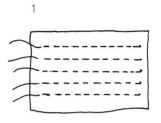

2

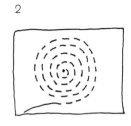

3

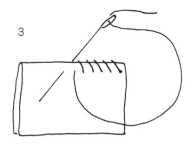

1. Running stitch: the heavier the fabric, the larger the stitch

2. Straight stitch worked in spiral from the centre out

3. Stitch worked over fold then pulled up

FABRIC FOLDING

Fold

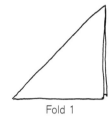

Fold 1

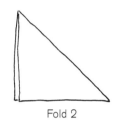

Fold 2

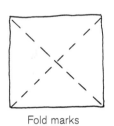

Fold marks

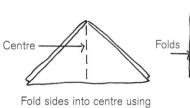

Centre ⟶

Fold sides into centre using fold marks as guide

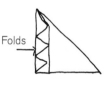

Folds

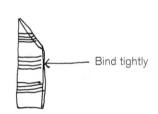

Bind tightly

BINDING FOR SHIBORI

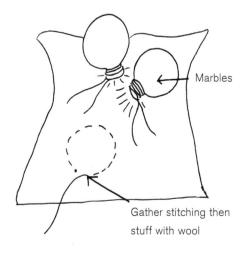

Marbles

Gather stitching then stuff with wool

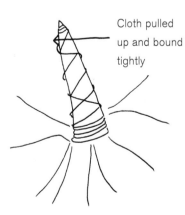

Cloth pulled up and bound tightly

Complete the felting process before dyeing. Dyeing can be carried out with acid dyes, either by steaming or in a microwave.

Another method of using shibori in conjunction with felt is to pattern cloth with shibori techniques and then felt onto the cloth, adding texture to the design. It is important to take shrinkage into account when working out the pattern, as it will reduce in scale during felting. It is possible to carry out more complex designs on cloth than on felt as cloth, being finer, is easier to manipulate.

__Below:__ Shibori on fine merino felt pieces illustrating a range of effects achieved by folding, tying and stitching. Resulting pieces stitched together in a patchwork effect.

Right: *Three-dimensional effect. Felt balls tied into white merino pre-felt and felted by agitating by hand in warm soapy water. After felting, acid dyes were applied to the surface using a syringe and steamed to set the dyes. Ties were removed after dyeing.*

Right: *Marbles tied into pre-felt of white merino on cotton scrim and felted by hand. Dyed in acid dye after felting but before ties were removed.*

Right: *Two fine layers of dull green merino wool pre-felted on to rainbow-dyed cotton scrim. Glass beads were tied into the pre-felt with the scrim on the top surface and felted by hand. After felting, the ties and beads were removed. Some of the resulting felt bubbles were cut into to reveal the layer of wool underneath. Surface stitching added.*

Texture with Nuno Felt

7 Texture with Nuno Felt

Nuno felt, a combination of felt with fabric, has opened up many design possibilities, leading to the production of innovative textiles. In this type of feltmaking, small quantities of wool fibres are placed on the surface of a lightweight fabric, either in a controlled design or randomly, according to the effect required. First the wool fibres are persuaded to work through to the reverse of the fabric, prior to felting. Then, as they felt, the fabric is pulled up with them, creating a ruched, textured effect. The results are lightweight, strong and drape beautifully. Different effects are obtained from different fabrics: the heavier the fabric, the greater the texture. Cotton muslin, for example, will create a more obvious texture than silk chiffon. Natural fabrics offer the possibility of creating more even textures than synthetics.

Previous spread: Nuno felt on rainbow-dyed cotton muslin.

CHOOSING MATERIALS FOR NUNO FELT

Ideally, you should use fabrics made from natural fibres that are lightweight and have a fairly open weave and a matt surface, such as cotton muslin, cotton scrim, silk chiffon, gauze or silk georgette. Shiny or synthetic fibres give interesting textures in small areas, but are not advisable for producing lengths, as the wool tends to slip over the surface rather than bonding to it. Use wools, prepared as tops, that are fine and quick-felting, such as merino, blue-faced Leicester or Shetland.

METHOD

1 Lay the chosen fabric on bubble wrap.
2 Place wool fibres on the fabric in the required design and cover them with net.
3 Sprinkle cool felting solution over the net.
4 Press the solution through the package and rub until the fibres and fabric are wet, then remove net.
5 Carry out the felting process, rolling in the usual way until it is possible to feel the wool fibres on the underside of the fabric, showing that they have penetrated through the fabric.
6 Fold the fabric into a package, with the wool on the inside, and rub with soap.
7 Throw the package gently on the table, approximately 20 to 30 times.
8 Open the package and refold it, with the folds in a different position. Repeat the throwing process. The wool will begin to shrink, due to the vibrations caused by throwing the fabric.

Right: Small circles of merino wool varying in sizes felted onto rainbow-dyed scrim. As the wool felts, the weave of the scrim distorts, producing interesting textures.

Left: A fine grid of merino fibres felted onto rainbow-dyed cotton muslin. The fabric is pulled up as the wool shrinks, and edges without wool become shaped by the movement of the felting wool.

9   Continue throwing until the wool begins to shrink. Once shrinking begins, the process can be speeded up by dipping the felt into hot water to increase the temperature before throwing. Continue in this way until the required result is obtained.

10 Rinse thoroughly and dry.

For functional purposes, maximum shrinkage should be aimed for (it is possible to shrink the felt down to half of the original size). For decorative purposes, this is not essential and the choice will be guided by the desired appearance.

Top tips

The most important factor in making this type of felt is to create a good bond between wool and fabric prior to felting. Start with cool water and only increase the temperature after the fibres have penetrated the fabric.

Keep the package wet and soapy during the throwing process to avoid causing the fibres to become fluffy on the surface.

An alternative method of increasing the temperature is to place the wet felt in a bowl and heat it in a microwave for 1 minute. Next, wearing rubber gloves to protect your hands from scalding, throw the felt until cool. Repeat the process as often as required.

DESIGNING WITH NUNO

The choice of fabric and method of applying the fibres will dictate the design. Wool fibres shrink back along their own length, so this needs to be taken into account when laying out the design. Using wool tops, in which the fibres lie parallel to each other, makes it easy to determine the fibre direction. Edges can be controlled by placing thin strips of wool tops close to the edge of the fabric. The wool works its way through the fabric and as it felts it retains the shape of the edge on which it was laid. This is particularly useful when a straight edge is desired. Shaped edges can be obtained by leaving the fabric edges free of wool, but arranging the pattern so that at intervals strips of wool lie at right angles to the edge. As the wool shrinks it pulls the fabric with it, and areas without wool are unaffected, resulting in a ruched or shaped edge. The fabric chosen will also affect the quality and type of texture. Fabrics made from natural fibres produce a more even texture, as wool fibres pass evenly through them, and shrinkage is even. Synthetic fabrics tend to be slippery due to the filaments from which they are made, and wool fibres have more difficulty in passing through. Often this happens unevenly – shrinkage is then uneven but often results in interesting surfaces.

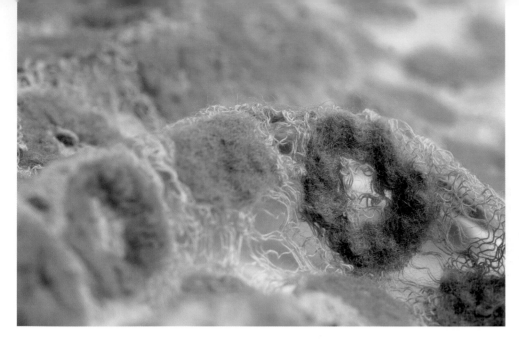

Left: Cotton scrim rainbow dyed in Procion dyes with fine lengths of merino tops formed into circles, giving a cell-like effect.

Textured nuno felt

For a first attempt at nuno felt, it is useful to lay the wool in a grid, as this gives a clear indication of the direction of felting. Measure the fabric before you start, so that you can calculate the amount by which it shrinks. Keep two opposite edges straight by positioning lengths of wool close to the edge of the fabric and to leave the other pair free of wool, which will result in a scalloped effect. This first sample can then become a reference for future experiments.

What you will need

Loom-state cotton muslin, approximately 50cm (20in) square
Bubble wrap
Merino wool tops
Dyed silk fibres

Method

1 Lay the muslin on bubble wrap.
2 Pull off a length of merino tops, equal to the length of the fabric.
3 One by one, separate thin strips, no thicker than a pencil, from the length of wool. Try to get each strip in one unbroken length; if this is not possible, you can join the ends by overlapping them when you place the wool on the fabric.
4 Lay out the thin wool strips in a grid, leaving spaces of at least 6–7cm (approximately 2½in) between them. You may vary the spacing if you choose. To make straight edges, place a wool strip along the fabric edge; for a scalloped effect, leave the edges of fabric uncovered.
5 Lay small quantities of dyed silk fibres on top of wool strips. This will increase the textured effect created when the silk is pulled up as the wool shrinks.
6 Felt the sample (see page 66), then measure your finished sample and calculate the rate of shrinkage.

Right: Silk georgette and merino wool, rainbow dyed with acid dyes after felting.

REVERSIBLE FABRICS

When nuno fabrics are produced by laying wools on one side of the fabric, the result is that one side will look very different to the other: the wool is visible on the surface on which it was placed, while only the ruched effect caused by the shrinking wool is visible on the reverse side. No particular side is the 'right' side; it is up to the maker to determine which will be chosen as the visible side.

For situations where both sides are going to be visible, it is possible to produce a reversible fabric. To do this, wool is applied to both sides of the fabric.

Method

1 Lay the fabric out on bubble wrap.
2 Apply wool fibres, using your chosen method of application.
3 Cover the layer with net and wet the fibres.
4 Remove the net and place a second piece of bubble wrap on top of the fabric.
5 Carefully turn the two layers of plastic over so that the bottom layer of bubble wrap ends up on top.
6 Remove the top sheet of bubble wrap. The fabric is now facing up, with the layer of wool underneath.
7 Apply a second layer of wool to this side and then wet and felt in the usual way.

Right: Tropicana coat (detail) – full-length evening coat. Nuno on silk chiffon dyed with Procion dyes. Wool was pre-felted to give more control when placing on the fabric. Synthetic threads, lace and shreds of metallic fibres were added to the pre-felt for texture.

Left: Double-sided design. White and brown blue-faced Leicester wool on reverse of rainbow-dyed silk chiffon. Outline pattern of brown tops on surface.

Pre-felts in Nuno

Increased control can be gained by pre-felting the fibres before application to the fabric. The pre-felt must be very thin and felted enough to keep its shape when applied to the fabric. You can incorporate fabric and yarn scraps into the pre-felt to add to the texture. Pre-felts can also be used to form decorative shaped edges.

DECORATIVE EDGES

The edges of felt self-seal as the wool fibres entangle in the felt-making process. This offers opportunities to shape edges without the need to find ways of preventing them from fraying. To design a shaped edge, it is necessary to make a template of the required design, making an allowance for subsequent shrinkage. Foam plastic sheeting, of the type sold as underlay for laminate floors, is good for this purpose, as it can be placed on wet felt without disintegrating.

The method is the same as that given for reversible fabric up to the point when the package has been turned over to bring the net to the top. At this stage, carefully lay prepared pre-felt on the edge of the net, leaving a small edging visible. If it is necessary to join pieces of pre-felt at the edging, then allow small overlaps. In this way, the wool will not leave gaps in the edging when it shrinks. When the edging is in place, cover it with net. Wet the wool and fabric and rub the edging in place with a little olive oil soap. Felt as usual until the layers are all firmly felted together, but have not yet started to shrink. At this point, carefully cut the edges, following the shape of the pre-felt, before completing the felting process.

Above: *Daisies. Units of very fine pre-felt on silk chiffon with surface beading.*

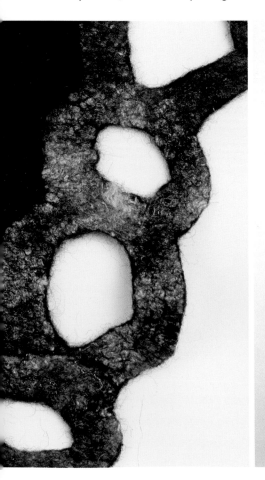

Left: *Decorative edges – pre-felt with surface layer of natural tussah silk. One layer of white wool on reverse of silk chiffon gauze, wetted out and turned over to bring the silk gauze to the surface. Pre-felts cut to shape using a previously designed template and placed on the surface of the fabric, felted until all layers were enmeshed but not shrinking. The edges of felt and centres of design were then cut away to match the pre-felts and the fabric was then completely felted.*

Far left: *Nuno scarf with decorative edge.*

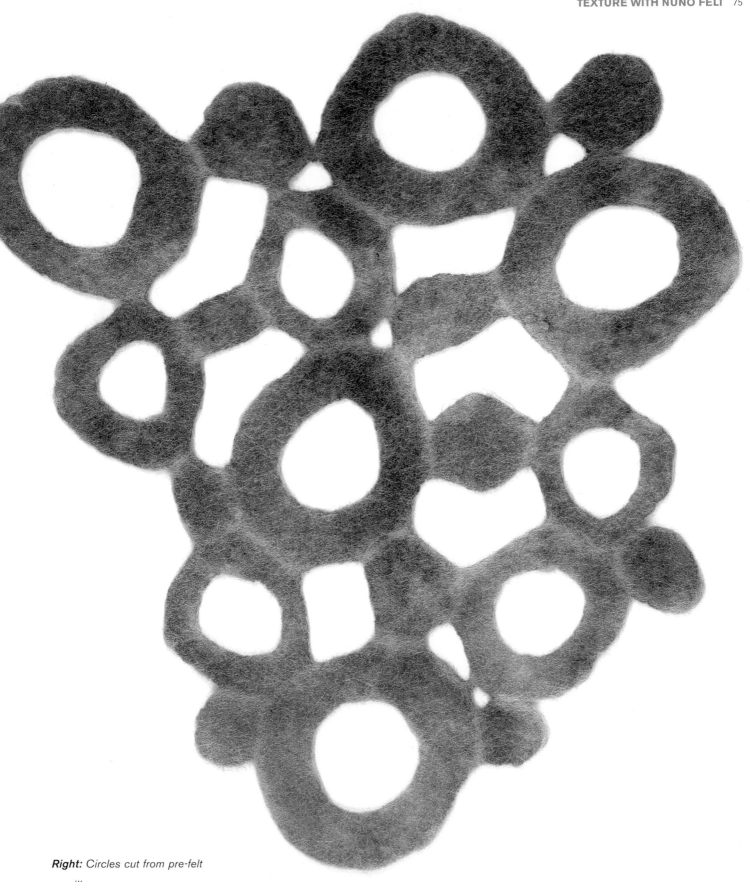

Right: *Circles cut from pre-felt on silk gauze.*

NUNO-FELTED FRAGMENTS

Nuno felt is versatile and ideal when a lightweight, but strong, felt is required, but it has the disadvantage of requiring considerable space for the making process, due to its potential shrinkage. Generally, nuno felt will shrink down to half its length and width. In other words, to achieve a finished measurement of 50cm (20in) square, you would require a 1m (40in) square of fabric. Breaking down a large project into small units or fragments makes it seem less daunting. Logistically, this makes the process easier, as it does not require so much space, which is a consideration to bear in mind if you do not have a dedicated space available. In this way, rather than trying to tackle the whole project at once, you can prepare fragments over a period of time. Inspiration can come from random patchwork designs or traditional crocheted motifs, in both of which techniques small units are assembled to make the whole.

Method

First prepare a series of nuno pre-felt pieces, making them in different sizes and using a range of techniques, such as those suggested below.

- Apply wool fibres very lightly to the fabric and add silk fibres as highlights.
- Make a sheet of fine pre-felt, using only two thin layers of fibre. Allow this to dry and then cut shapes from it and apply these to the fabric.
- If controlled edges are required, apply fibres lightly to both the right and wrong sides of each edge.
- Edges of pre-felt, extended beyond the fabric, can be stretched and manipulated during felting to produce interesting effects.

Whichever technique is chosen, the wool applied to the fabric should be partially felted until it has made its way through to the reverse of the fabric. If you are preparing the pieces over a period of time, rinse each finished piece carefully, and then dry, iron and store it until required. Once several fragments have been prepared, consider how they will be joined. Play with them, rearranging them until you are satisfied with the result.

Combining the fragments

1 Overlap the edges of pieces to be joined.
2 Insert a thin layer of wool fibre between the overlapped fabric edges. If there are many pieces or if the shapes are complex, it is useful to join the edges at this point. This may be done with basting stitches or using a fine felting needle to needle them together, as described on page 116. (If the base fabric is silk

Above: Nuno fragments. This piece was constructed from three separate strips of nuno felt. If careful thought is given to the design of each strip, joins can be almost invisible.

chiffon, it is better to stitch pieces together, as the felting needles tend to snag the fabric.)

3 Wet the fragments with felting solution, rubbing the joins gently to start the felting process.

4 Roll until the wool has penetrated both pieces and the join is secure. Next, remove any basting stitches, wet the whole piece and throw it in the usual way to complete nuno felting.

5 Rinse the finished piece and leave it to dry.

NUNO IN THREE DIMENSIONS

If the fabric to be incorporated into nuno felt is first shaped and stitched, it is possible to produce a three-dimensional piece. A favourite project is a simple decorative bag, such as a small evening purse or a small gift bag, designed to turn a gift into something special.

Left: Gift bag. Two fine layers of merino fibres sandwiched between a top layer of dyed silk georgette and a lower layer of silk chiffon. The heavier weight of the georgette enhances the texture.

Below: Double-sided nuno silk and felt purse.

Double nuno gift bag

Method

1 Make a pattern for the finished size and shape of bag.

2 Enlarge this by two thirds, both vertically and horizontally.

3 Cut a template from plastic foam sheeting to this enlarged size.

4 Cut four layers of fabric to the size of template, plus ½cm (¼in) turnings on all sides. (The fabric is to be used double, so the four layers will be stitched together to form two bags.)

5 Draw the stitching line on the fabric with a water-soluble marker pen.

6 Baste each bag around the stitching line, leaving the top edge open.

7 Machine stitch the seams and then trim the seam allowances fairly close to the stitching.

8 Place one bag over the plastic template, with raw edges on the outside.

9 Baste the top edge closed, so that plastic is completely enclosed.

10 With the bag flat, lay a fringe of fibres around the sides and lower edge, and then lay a layer of merino fibres on the upper side.

11 Cover with net, wet out with felting solution, then flatten the fibres and gently rub a bar of soap over the surfaces. Rub just enough to hold the fibres in position (the extra soap acts as a temporary 'glue').

12 Remove the net and turn the bag over. Turn in the fringe and lay a layer of fibres over this side of bag. Wet the fibres and rub gently as before, then remove the net.

13 Carefully pull the second fabric bag over the first. This time, the seams should be in the inside.

14 Add more water/soap, if necessary, and rub to make the layers stick together.

15 Add pre-felted shapes to decorate the outside.

16 Continue felting by rolling the bag in bubble wrap around a wooden dowel. Keep the package wet and soapy.

17 When the felt begins to shrink and the plastic distorts, carefully remove the basting stitches from the top edge and slide out the plastic template.

18 Continue rolling until the wool fibres are firmly though the fabric.

19 Continue felting by throwing. This should be done cold at first and then, if necessary, the felt can be heated up with hot water until the required size is achieved.

20 Rinse out the soap, squeezing to remove as much water as possible. Pull the bag into shape and allow it to dry.

21 To complete the bag, add handles made from twisted cords or stitch eyelets around the top edge and thread ribbon or cord through to draw it up. The addition of beads or tassels would enhance the feeling of opulence.

FELT AND FABRICS

Combining felt with fabric opens up many possibilities for design. Felting on to a range of fabrics can produce widely differing results. The one constant is that the fabric will ruche up to some degree, but the extent to which this happens will depend on several factors:

- the weight and fibre content of the fabric
- the structure of the fabric
- the quantity of wool and method of application

Lightweight cottons such as muslin are excellent for this technique. An even layer of wool, when applied to muslin, will result in a all-over fine texture. Applying the wool more randomly will result in some areas being gathered and some flat.

Above: Patchwork silk sample. Strips are cut and stitched together either with tacking threads (removed after felting) or large decorative stitches. Further surface stitching was added after felting.

Silk chiffon gauze is ideal for lightweight but strong felts. Chiffon is often used as a backing for the felt, as it allows the felted layer to be very fine. The heavier the fabric, the more pronounced the texture will be. Interesting patchwork effects result from joining different fabrics together before felting.

Patchwork method

1 First draw the shape for the finished piece. Allow for 50 per cent shrinkage in each direction.
2 Divide the area into strips or sections.
3 Cut up the drawing and use the pieces as patterns for each section.
4 Cut the pieces out of fabric, adding a narrow seam allowance on all sides where joins will be needed.
5 Assemble the pieces, overlapping the edges where two pieces meet.
6 Pin and baste, to hold the pieces in position.
7 Stitch the pieces together by hand, using a variety of threads and stitches.
8 Remove basting threads.
9 Lay the fabric patchwork face down on bubble wrap and apply two very fine layers of fibre to the reverse side.
10 Wet and felt by first rolling and, finally, throwing.

Simple patchwork techniques can also be used as a method of breaking down a large area of felt into manageable sections. This is suitable for both wearable and decorative pieces. Pre-felts are used in this method.

Right: Double-sided nuno; black merino wool on silk chiffon with a surface of dyed silk tops.

Making felted patchwork designs with pre-felt: method one

1   Sketch the required design (perhaps for a cushion, bag, hanging or item of clothing) on paper. Draw the patchwork shapes of each section, keeping them simple and avoiding too many small patches.

2   Scale this sketch up on paper to double the required finished size: for example, a finished size of 30cm (12in) square needs to be scaled up to 60cm (24in).

3   Number the patches on both the original sketch and the scaled-up version.

4   Cut out the paper patches from the scaled-up plan and divide them into groups, according to which pre-felt they will be made from. Allow 6mm (¼in) allowances to account for overlapping.

5   Lay out each group of patches together and measure the total area of each group (vertical and horizontal measurements).

6   Make the sheets of pre-felt according to instructions on page 39.

7   One by one, lay the sheets of pre-felt face down on bubble wrap. Cover each with silk chiffon, wet it and continue to felt. As the felt shrinks, watch carefully until it is nearly as small as required. At this point, stop.

8   Pin the pattern pieces (the ones for the finished size) in place on the felt and cut out to shape, but leaving 6–12mm (¼–½in) of felt extending beyond the pattern.

9   Remove the pattern and continue felting until the final size is reached.

10   Rinse, dry and press into shape.

11   Assemble the patchwork pieces, slightly overlapping the edges, and stitch in position, either by hand or machine.

Right and below: Waistcoat: merino wool on reverse of fine cotton lawn with design on surface of the lawn. Textured surface is due to contraction of the fabric as the wool shrinks.

WAISTCOAT

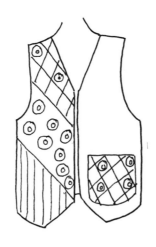

Right front constructed from three sections felted to size and joined by machine stitching.

THREE SECTIONS

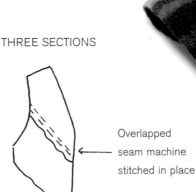

Overlapped seam machine stitched in place

Making felted patchwork designs with pre-felt: method two

1 Follow Method One up to the end of step 6.

2 Stitch the pre-felted patches together by hand or machine. If stitching by hand, either make small over-sewing stitches on the reverse, using matching cotton, or make larger stitches on the right side, using threads of heavier weight. If you are stitching by machine, use a large zigzag stitch with uneven tension between top and bottom threads (so that the stitching can be removed easily).

3 Press the stitched piece and then lay it face down on bubble wrap and proceed as in Step 7 of Method One. Remove any machine stitches.

4 Finally, place the pattern for the final piece on top of the patchwork and cut out the final piece.

Three-Dimensional Felt: Hollow Forms

8 Three-Dimensional Felt: Hollow Forms

This method of felt-making exploits the unique capability of wool to form seams without the need for stitching, which makes it possible to construct three-dimensional hollow forms without joins. As there are no seams, it will not be possible to adjust the dimensions after felting is complete. It is therefore important to consider the shrinkage rate of the wool during the felting process and make allowances for this when laying out the fibres. To prevent the two sides from felting together, fibres are laid out around both sides of a template of the desired shape and size.

Templates

Templates are usually made from plastic, as the wool will not stick to the surface. The plastic used should be thick enough to allow you to feel the outline when building up the shape. Such templates have the advantage of being reusable. Plastic of the type used by builders to place under concrete floors is suitable, but the best material is the foam sheeting sold in DIY stores as underlay for laminate floors. This foam has a textured surface that prevents the fibres from slipping. It also has the advantage of being lightweight and easy to handle. When making the templates, an allowance for shrinkage must be added to the planned size of the project.

Calculating shrinkage

First make a paper pattern of the planned shape and note down all the measurements. The average allowance for shrinkage in this type of feltmaking is 40 per cent. A simple method of calculating the shrinkage is as follows:

1 Making a note of all measurements, first measure the required height of the finished article. Next, measure the width. If the sides are not straight, measure the widest and narrowest points.
2 For rounded shapes, measure the circumference and divide this measurement in half.
3 To calculate the allowance:

$$\frac{\text{height} \times 4}{10} = \text{amount to be added to height for shrinkage}$$

$$\frac{\text{width or half circumference} \times 4}{10} = \text{amount to be added to width for shrinkage}$$

4 Add the amount required for shrinkage to each of the original measurements to arrive at the measurements required for the template.

Choosing a suitable fibre

Hollow forms need to be sufficiently robust to retain their shape. The choice of fibre will depend on the intended end use. The larger the shape, the stronger the fibre that will be required to support it. Below are some fibre suggestions.

Small bags − merino; blue-faced Leicester; Shetland

Larger bags − Gotland; black Welsh; Swaledale

Hats − merino; blue-faced Leicester

Slippers − Icelandic; finn wool

HOW TO BEGIN

1 Calculate the required measurements of the finished piece. If you are using an object as a starting point, measure the height and width.
2 Cut out a paper pattern to the desired size. To calculate height, measure from the top to the middle of the base; to calculate width, measure the circumference and divide by two. Calculate shrinkage (see opposite).
3 Make a template from plastic, including the allowance for shrinkage.

Right: Line drawings of pattern and template measurements for three-dimensional seamless purses.

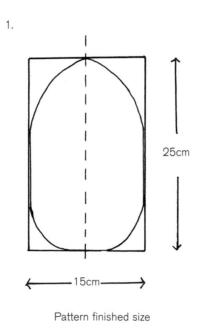

1.

25cm

←————15cm————→

Pattern finished size

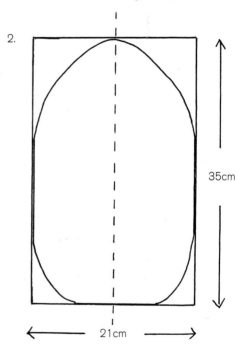

2.

35cm

←————— 21cm —————→

Template with 40 per cent shrinkage allowance

4   Set out your work table as usual. Place the template flat on the bubble wrap and then lay a fringe of fibres all around the template, with the fibres extending half over the edge (see diagram opposite).

5   Lay down a vertical layer of fibres, from edge to edge of template (see diagram).

6   Place a second layer of fibres at right angles to the first, taking the second layer only to the edge of the template (see diagram).

7   Cover the fibres with net and wet as usual. Sprinkle felting solution in the centre and work the water out towards the edge of template. Try to keep the fringe dry.

8   Remove the net and turn the template over.

9   Turn the fringes in over the edge, wetting the template, if necessary, to hold the fibres in place (see diagram).

10   Position a vertical layer of fibres just within the template.

11   Make a fringe of fibres around the template.

12   Place a horizontal layer of fibres in position (see diagram).

13   Cover the fibres with net and wet as before and then remove the net, turn template over and turn in the fringes. The template is now covered with two layers of fibre on each side.

14   Lay a fringe around the edge and fill in with a vertical layer of fibres. Wet these in the usual way and turn the template.

15   Turn the fringe over and fill in with a vertical layer. The template is now covered with three layers of fibre.

16   Some form of decoration may be added at this stage.

Depending on the required end use, three layers of fibres might be sufficient. For example, this is enough for small bags, small vessels, hats and so on. For larger bags, slippers, boots and similar items, further layers might be required. The number of layers will be determined by the end use, as will the choice of wool type.

The success or failure of this type of feltmaking depends upon careful placing of the fibres and then the care taken during the first stages of hand felting, prior to any rolling. First, harden the edges of the package by folding the bubble wrap over the edges and rubbing while pushing the fibres back against the edges of the template. Next, harden the surface by rubbing over the bubble wrap. Only when the package feels firm, with no wrinkles, should the main felting process begin. Starting to roll too early causes the fibres to stretch out over the edges of the template and can result in unwanted felted ridges.

Right: *Fibre layout for a three-dimensional purse.*

LAYING OUT FIBRES AROUND A TEMPLATE

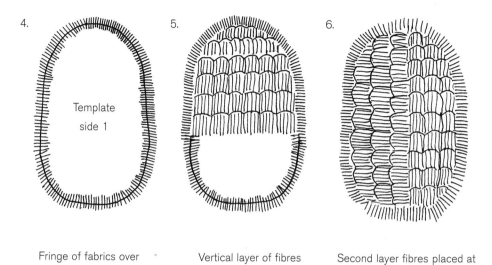

4. Fringe of fabrics over edge of template

5. Vertical layer of fibres to cover template

6. Second layer fibres placed at right angles to first layer

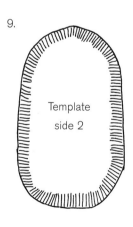

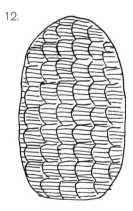

9. Fringe from side 1 turned over edge of template to side 2

12. Side 2 covered with two layers of fibres, giving two layers all around the template

FELTING THE FIBRES

1 The process is carried out as for flat felt, but when the fibres are beginning to felt you must cut the opening to release the template.

2 Rub the cut edges with soapy fingers to seal the layers of fibres together and then insert one hand inside the layers of felt and rub the folded edge with soap to ensure that no ridges are formed.

3 Remove the template and resume rolling on the bamboo mat. Change the position of the sides to avoid making ridges. Roll 50 times in each direction and on both sides.

4 Turn the felt inside out and repeat the rolling. Continue in this way until the felt has shrunk down to the size of the original pattern.

5 Rinse to remove all soap. Shape the felt by hand. Stuff the shape with crumpled newspaper and allow it to dry.

If the felt is to be blocked into a particular shape, for hats or moulded vessels and so on, steam it over a boiling kettle and stretch it on to the block. Leave it on the block to dry.

A SEAMLESS FELT PURSE

This is a good introduction to seamless felting. Choose a simple shape and work systematically through the process. The purses illustrated here were all made from the same template. Variations were obtained by choosing different fibres and by cutting into the fibres in different positions.

The pattern

The finished size of the purse is 15cm (6in) wide and 25cm (10in) long, the pattern length including the flap and the depth of the purse.

1 Cut the paper pattern to size. An easy way to do this is to start by drawing a rectangle equal to the length and width of the pattern.

2 Mark the width in half at the top and bottom and draw in this line.

3 On one side of the rectangle, draw in the shape of one half of the purse.

4 Fold the paper in half down the centre line and cut out the purse shape, cutting around the drawn outline. This method will ensure that the two sides match.

A useful tip when designing the pattern: the lower corners should be rounded off to prevent ugly points developing during the felting process.

To make the template

The template needs to be 40 per cent larger than the pattern, to allow for shrinkage during felting. With the addition of this 40 per cent allowance, the original pattern measurements become 21 x 35cm (8¼ x 14in).

1 Draw a rectangle to these measurements and repeat the process used for the pattern to draw the template shape.
2 Cut the template shape from paper.
3 Place the paper template on plastic sheet; draw round the edge with a permanent marker pen and cut out the template.

Right: *Purse made from rainbow-dyed merino wool with silk sari yarn as decoration on the flap. Also shows paper pattern, finished size and plastic template, with 40% allowance for shrinkage added to the original pattern measurement.*

Making the purse

1 Lay out the fibres (see pages 88–89).

2 Harden the edges and surface of the felt by hand, as described.

3 When the package feels firm, roll it in the usual way.

4 As the felt begins to shrink, the package will begin to curl at the edges when the wool becomes smaller than the template. When this happens, it is time to open the package.

5 Decide the position of the opening and cut carefully into the felt at this point.

6 Treat the cut edges as described on page 90 and continue felting.

7 Check the size of the felt against the original pattern and continue felting until the required size is reached.

8 Rinse and then spin out excess water. Pull the felt into shape and leave it to dry.

9 If required, the shape can be maintained during drying by stuffing the purse with crumpled newspaper.

Blocking

The dry purse now requires blocking to help the shape to become permanent. This is done by pressing the inside of the felt with a moderate iron, either with steam or with a damp cloth. A travelling iron is ideal for this operation, as its small size will make it easier to manoeuvre inside the purse.

1 Starting with the base, steam press to make the felt hot and damp and therefore more malleable. Using a heavy hammer or meat-tenderizing mallet, hammer the felt on a hard surface until you have achieved the desired shape.

2 Repeat the process to form the sides of the purse.

Finishing the purse

When finishing felted items, it is important that suitable materials and processes are chosen. If you are using commercial fastenings, cords and the like, choose them sensitively, so that they complement the felt. Fastenings, cords and decorations can all be made from felt.

Below: Purse made from a mix of natural black Welsh mountain and blue-faced Leicester fleece. The decoration on the flap is rainbow-dyed tussah silk.

Left and right: *Vessels by Jenny Pepper – hand-moulded hollow bowls using carded Gotland wool, embellished with natural pebbles collected while walking.* **Left:** Boulder III; **right:** Coppice II.

Finishes for Felt

9 Finishes for Felt

As with every craft, the final finish of a felt-making project is vital. Poor finishing or ill-matched fastenings and decorations can ruin an otherwise successful project. It is important, when selecting trimmings and finishes for felt articles, that materials that will suit the felt are chosen in place of inappropriate commercial finishes. Cords, beads and buttons can themselves be made from felt and these are the most suitable type to use for felt articles.

A FELT CORD

Cords can be couched in position as surface decoration, applied as a piping around cushions and other articles and used as straps for bags.

What you will need

Wool tops in suitable colours
Bowl of warm soapy water
Bamboo mat

Method

1 Measure length of required cord and add 30 per cent for shrinkage (see diagram).
2 Select the wool tops to be used. To assess the thickness of the finished cord, twist the dry tops tightly in your hand. This will give a good indication of the diameter of the finished cord.
3 Pull off the required length and width. Choose just one colour or make a mixture.
4 Holding the dry tops in one hand, dip the other hand into the bowl of soapy water and squeeze one end of the tops' length to make it damp. Repeat this several times, until approximately 30cm (12in) of the length is damp.
5 Roll between the hands until they begin to form a soft roll (see diagram).
6 Continue down the whole length of the tops in this way.
7 Return to the first end and gradually repeat the process, wetting the fibres and continuing to roll on the bamboo mat until the whole length is wet (see diagram).
8 Roll the cord gently on the bamboo mat, working on one section at a time.
9 Continue until the whole length has had this treatment.
10 Wet and roll as required, increasing the pressure of the rolling to compact the cord. More rolling between the hands or on the bamboo mat will help to make the cord firm and resistant to pilling in use.
11 Rinse and dry.

Previous spread: Merino wool hand-rolled into felt balls, alternated with ceramic beads to form a necklace.

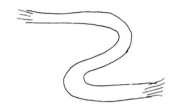

1. Pull strip from the wool tops the required width and length, plus allowance for shrinkage

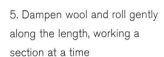

5. Dampen wool and roll gently along the length, working a section at a time

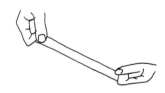

7. Check width and roll until firm

Right: Felt Identities by Linda Hume. Felt balls were first wet-felted then embellished with dry-felted details using felting needles, and finally with beadwork.

A FELT BALL

Balls made of layers of different colours and thoroughly felted can be cut through the centre, when dry, to reveal multi-coloured layers. Various shapes can be created using the method described below. If balls are to be cut and used as fastenings, they should be sealed with diluted PVA glue to preserve the shape and prevent the cut surface from wearing away.

What you will need

A selection of wool tops
Small bowl of warm soapy water
Bamboo mat
Dry felting needle
Piece of plastic foam, at least 5cm (2in) thick

Method

There are several methods that can be used to make a felt ball, but this is one of the simplest. It involves the use of a felting needle, which should be handled with care.

1   Pull off lengths of tops of approximately 60cm (24in) and split lengthways into three or four strips.
2   Wind one of these strips tightly around a finger.
3   Remove the fibre from the finger and wind a second strip of wool tightly over it, as if winding a ball of knitting yarn.
4   Place the dry ball of wool on the foam pad and carefully and gently stick the felting needle in and out of the mass of fibres (see diagram). Work around the fibre until it forms a soft ball shape. The ball will diminish in size as it shrinks and compresses, so make allowances for this. If the sizing of the ball is critical, then it is wise to make some samples first to help you decide how large the ball needs to be before felting.
5   Continue winding fibres on as before and needling lightly to hold them in position. Different colours may be used for the different layers, if desired.
6   Once the ball is large enough, dip it into the bowl of warm soapy water and turn it around so that only the surface fibres get wet.
7   Remove from the water and gently roll it between the fingers and palms of the hand. It is important that only light pressure is exerted at this point.
8   As the wool begins to felt, the ball should be dipped into the water again and the rolling pressure increased, to compact the fibres.
9   Continue in this way, wetting and rolling until the ball is felted through and through.
10 Rinse and dry.

MAKING A BALL

4. Use a felting needle to gently prod the outer edges of the ball

Above: *Felt jewellery and balls.*

TOGGLES

Toggle-like fastenings can be made from small pieces of felt. The felt is cut into squares or rectangles, rolled up tightly and then held in position with a stitch. Next, the roll is dipped in diluted PVA and allowed to dry. These toggles can be stitched in position with a strong buttonhole thread.

LOW-RELIEF DESIGNS

Another use for cords and felted balls is to insert them within the layers of dry fibre when making felt in order to produce low-relief designs. As the cords and balls are already felted, they do not shrink further while this new felt is made. If the felt is worked on flat, the top layer of new felt can be made to adhere to the already felted shapes, producing a felt with a low relief design. Surface stitching can be added to enhance the effect. In the samples illustrated, the felt was made from white merino and acid dyes were applied with syringes after felting. The stitching was added last.

Right: Felt balls, cut in half, and felt cord inserted between layers of merino and felted to produce a low-relief motif. Wool was subsequently dyed. Machine stitching outlines and defines the design.

Left: Thick felt cords felted between layers with surface stitching. Rainbow dyed after felting but before stitches were applied.

Surface Pattern on Felt

10 Surface Pattern on Felt

Simple colouring methods can be used to create surface design on felt. When preparing felt for surface patterning, it is best to use merino fibre and felt it thoroughly, producing a dense, firm surface on which to work.

Suitable techniques include stencilling and printing with blocks. Designs should be simple, without too much detail, as the slightly fuzzy surface of felt will in any case disguise detail.

Various colouring materials may be used, including fabric paints, widely available from craft suppliers, and paint sticks. Markal Paintstiks, used here, are thick chunky crayons in which the pigment is mixed with oil and wax. The colour is moist and easy to apply.

USING MARKAL PAINTSTIKS

The crayons can be applied directly to the felt and the colour is then worked in with a stencil brush or toothbrush. Shading can be built up with the application of more than one colour, giving a variety of tones and colours. A particularly useful technique is to apply masking tape to the surface of the felt, rub the Paintstik on the masking tape and then spread the colour outwards on to the felt with a toothbrush. The resulting combination of clear, sharp edges where the tape ends and soft blended areas where the colour is spread is particularly effective.

After application, the colour must be left to set for 48 hours and the felt should then be ironed, to seal the colour.

Previous spread: Fraction V *(Jackie Lunn). Inlaid pre-felts with additional details applied with a felting needle.*

Left: *Markal Paintstiks.*

STENCILLING

Commercially prepared stencils are available, but it is easy to make your own. Various materials may be used to make stencils. Cardboard from cereal packets is ideal, as the coated side of the card prolongs the life of the stencil. Sticky-backed plastic, sheets of special stencil plastic or even masking tape can also be used.

To make a stencil, draw the shape to be cut on to the card or plastic. If you are using sticky-backed plastic or cereal packets, remember to draw the design in reverse. Place the stencil on a cutting mat and carefully cut the shape required, using a fine craft knife.

Prepare the felt for stencilling by placing it on a board or on the table and holding it taut with masking tape around the edges. Place the stencil in position and apply colour carefully. Markal Paintstiks can be used, as described opposite. Alternatively, fabric paints are widely available in metallic and non-metallic colours. These should be applied with a stencil brush.

Right: Stencil on scrim felted on merino wool. Handmade stencil and fabric paints, set with an iron.

PRINTING

Printing, in its simplest form, is a useful method for decorating the surface of felt. Blocks can be made from card, string or potatoes and are also available commercially. The printing block must have a raised surface and be rigid enough to stay in position when pressed.

The simplest type of block is one made from cardboard and string. The card needs to be rigid and quite thick and the string tightly spun, so that it doesn't flatten while in use.

A card and string block

1 Draw the required design on the card with a black pen.
2 Cut the card to the largest dimensions of the design.
3 Cover the surface of the card with double-sided tape.
4 Remove the covering from the double-sided tape.
5 Carefully place the string in position, making sure it remains tightly twisted.
6 Coat the surface of the block with acrylic varnish or PVA glue to make it more durable.

Above: White merino felt with experiments – used as a felt sketchbook.

Left: Merino wool felt with stitch and print. Some stitches added at the pre-felt stage, fully felted and dyed. Further stitching added and spirals printed with metallic fabric print using a handmade string block.

Right: Decorative felt with rich textures (Sarah Lawrence). Different contours on the surface created by free-machine stitch. Gilding and beadwork add to the opulent feel.

11 Cobweb Felt

As its name suggests, cobweb felt is light and airy but strong. It can be used on its own for fashion garments and applied as surface decoration to more robust felt.

Choosing suitable fibres

Fibres need to be fine and from a breed known to felt well, such as merino or Shetland. The wool should be prepared as a combed top. Fine lengths of wool or silk fibres can be added for strength.

Preparing the work area

1 Place a towel on the work surface.
2 Lay a bamboo blind on the towel. The blind should be as long and wide as the felt to be made (or as large as available).
3 Place a length of bubble wrap flat on the mat, making sure that it is smooth side up. It is essential that this is the full length of the planned felt.
4 Have a sheet of thin plastic available (these can be purchased from DIY stores).

MAKING COBWEB FELT

1 Break off a length of the chosen fibre. If possible, this should be as long as the felt to be made. For example, if you are making a scarf, it is best to start with tops that are the required length for the scarf, plus an allowance for shrinkage.
2 Place the wool top on the bubble wrap and, starting at one end, gradually spread the fibres out sideways. It is best to concentrate on one area at a time and handle the fibres gently, to avoid gaps appearing between the fibres and to prevent them crossing over each other. Continue in this way until all the fibres have been opened into a very fine even web.
3 Check the whole length and, if it is still not fine enough, continue to spread the fibres until you are satisfied with the result.
4 To add strength, place occasional fine lengths of wool or silk fibres at right angles.
5 Cover the fibres with net and wet them. Rub the surface of the net to start the felting process, but make sure that fibres do not work through the net.
6 Carefully remove the net and cover the fibres with thin plastic sheeting.
7 Roll the fibres and sheeting up tightly in bubble wrap, tie securely at both ends and roll firmly 100 times.
8 Open the bubble wrap, straighten the felt and then roll it up from the opposite end. Roll firmly a further 100 times.

9 Open the roll and straighten the fibres. Fold the web carefully, so that it can be turned through 90 degrees to fit into the width of the plastic.

10 Roll again 100 times then open, straighten, refold, turn package and repeat 100 rolls from the opposite side.

11 Remove the felt from the bubble wrap and place it on the bamboo blind.

12 Roll the felt 50 times from each side (200 rolls in all).

The next stage is to stretch the felt. Note that if the felt is long, you will need assistance to complete this stage.

Stretching

1 Roll one end of the web into one end of the mat and hold it firmly.

2 Roll the other end of the web into the opposite end of the mat.

3 With whoever is helping you, pull evenly on both ends of the mat. If the felt is shorter than the blind, the web will stretch. If the felt is longer than the mat, it should be folded before stretching, as the stretching process will only work if the web is shorter than the mat.

Completing the process

Below: Multi-coloured cobweb felted as decoration in white merino felt.

1 Wet the felt. Rub it with soap and continue rolling and stretching until the web is strong. During this process, holes may appear, but these are an acceptable part of the effect.

2 Complete the process by throwing the felt gently.

3 Give the felt a final stretch before rinsing and drying.

Cobweb felt as surface decoration

1 Carry out the process until the fibres have been rolled 400 times in bubble wrap.

2 Stretch the felt by hand to encourage open areas to appear.

3 Apply this to the surface of unfelted fibres and continue the process of felting.

12 Needle-Punched Felt

An industrial process in which felt is produced by means of special needles, without moisture or friction, is now becoming popular with felt makers. In the industry, the product is referred to as *non-woven* and has widely varying applications, such as tennis-court surfaces, tennis-ball covers, insulation and motor-vehicle carpeting. To produce the non-woven batt (web of fibres), fibres are carded into a thick web and passed under a machine with a needle board into which are inserted thousands of felting needles. These needles have small barbs at the pointed end and as they are repeatedly raised and lowered through the web, the fibres become interlocked. The resulting material can be used as a base for design and the whole piece wet-felted to produce a true felt.

Hand felting needles are now readily available in a range of sizes. They are used to produce dry felt sculptures (including felt balls; see page 100), to join pieces (see page 76) or to create designs by needling fibres or pre-felts, either to a base of machine-made needle-punched felt or to hand-rolled pre-felt. Felting needles can be used individually for adding fine details to a design or, for larger projects, several may be set into a hand-held tool.

Health and safety

- Felting needles should be handled carefully.
- The points and barbs are sharp and should be covered at all times when not in use.
- Use a cork to cover the point of a single needle.
- Store unused needles in a box.

Previous spread: Shapes cut from top layer of pre-felt and contrasting fibres applied from underneath with a felting needle.

Above: a felting needle. The point of the needle penetrates the layers of fibre. The barbs pick up fibres on the way down and push them through the lower layers. On the way up, lower fibres are pulled up again. As a result, fibre layers become entangled.

Right: Black merino felt with metallic threads and fancy yarns alternating with silver lurex fabric. Strips were machine stitched to a base of white needle-punched felt, which has been wet-felted.

USING FELTING NEEDLES AS DESIGN TOOLS

Work on a base of thick polystyrene sheet or foam rubber, placed on a table at a comfortable height for sitting. The base needs to be deep enough to prevent the needle from penetrating all the way through and hitting the table underneath. Polystyrene insulating foam can be obtained from builders' merchants.

Choose a needle that is suitable for your chosen project. Needle sizes range from size 19 gauge, for use with very coarse fibres, to 40 gauge, for fine work. The 36 gauge is a good general-purpose needle.

Basic method

1 Cut a piece of needle-punched felt or hand-rolled pre-felt, making sure it is large enough for the planned design and allowing for shrinkage when it is wet-felted.

2 Plan out the design and mark the main points with a water-soluble pen.

3 Cut out the required shapes from pre-felt, using fine pieces from tops or wool rovings. Place the design elements in position and needle them into position. The needles should be held firmly and steadied by holding the first finger braced against the shank of the needle, to give extra control. Holding the needle upright, push it down into the background and pull it back out of the felt.

4 Repeat this movement, developing a steady rhythm until each pattern piece is held in position.

5 To complete the design, place it on a second layer of needle-punched felt or add two fine layers of fibre to the back.

6 Wet and felt in the usual way.

Left: Needle-felted sample. Pre-felt with design cut out using a fine scalpel on a cutting board. Sample then laid face down on thick polystyrene sheet and fibres placed across the open shapes and held in place by lightly needling with a felting needle. Two further fine layers of Merino fibres laid across the surface and lightly needled to hold in position. The felting needle pushed the unfelted fibres through the pre-felted layer, producing spots of colour to break up the uniform surface. The whole was then fully felted.

LAYERS OF COLOUR WITH FELTING NEEDLES

Interesting effects can be achieved by using felting needles to layer colours.

What you will need

Sheets of pre-felt

Sharp scalpel or craft knife with small blade

Polystyrene or rubber foam pad

Wool tops, rovings, silk fibres or small fabric pieces

Cutting mat

Rotary cutter

Metal ruler

Felting needles

Method

1 Prepare several sheets of pre-felt, in contrasting colours.

2 Work out the design to be cut from one sheet of pre-felt. Place the felt on the cutting mat and carefully cut out the required design, using a small, sharp scalpel.

3 Place the felt with cutouts face down on a foam pad.

4 Select small pieces of wool tops or pre-felt in contrasting colours and place these over the holes. Needle them lightly into position.

5 Turn the felt right side up on the foam pad and add further details, using wool tops, rovings, silk fibres or small fabric pieces. Needle these lightly into position.

6 Turn felt again, laying it wrong side up on the foam, and place either a second layer of pre-felt over the back or thin layers of wool tops. Needle into position. Note that the needling pushes some of the background colour through the surface layer, breaking up the areas of plain colour. Needle as much or as little as required to achieve the effect you are happy with.

Right: Fragment V *(Jackie Lunn).*
Layers of colour with details applied using a felting needle and incorporating both hand and machine stitching.

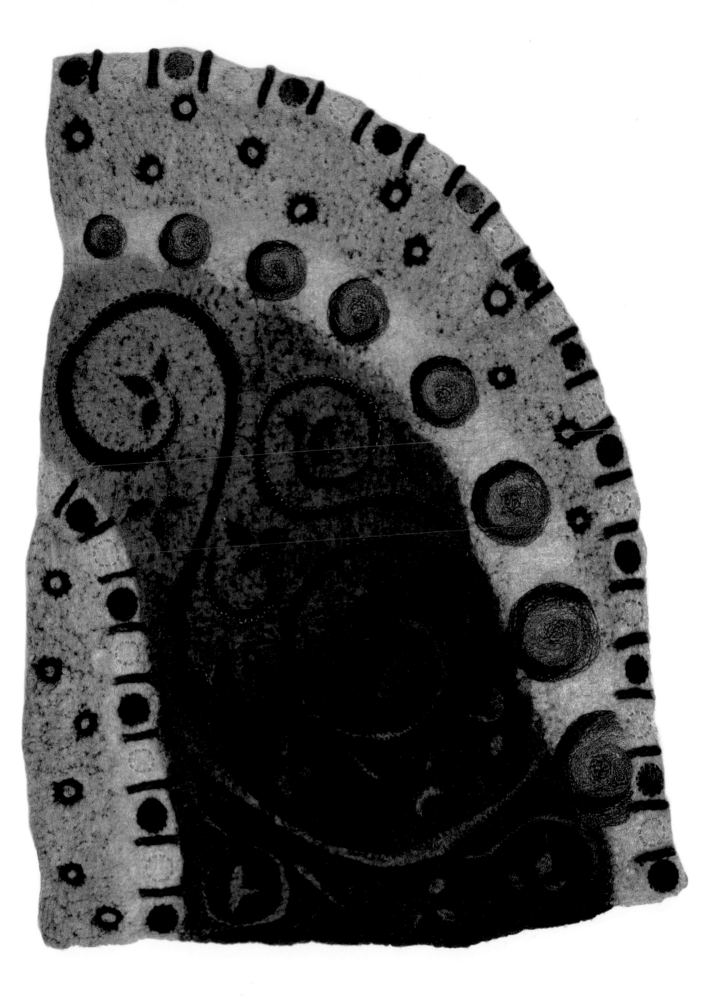

Conclusion

The felting of wool is a magical process, and the processes outlined in these pages will hopefully open your eyes to the endless possibilities for creating innovative fabrics. The explanations of the various processes are intended to give an understanding of what happens when wool felts, and the various ideas outlined here are just a beginning, a foundation on which to build your own experiments, giving you the confidence with which to design your own highly individual textiles. Happy felting!

Above: *Traditional Kyrgyz shirdak* felt.

Glossary of Useful Terms

Batt: web of fibres prepared commercially by carding machinery. Alternatively, the term given to short lengths of wool fibres pulled from combed tops, placed side by side to form several layers prior to felting.

Blending: mixing fibres of different colours or different types together.

Bradford count: measurement of the fineness of wool fibres. Based on a traditional system used by hand spinners and weavers (the higher the count, the finer the fibres).

Carders: equipment for separating wool fibres or blending different types or colours of wool. Carders have fine wires set in leather or synthetic rubber cloth attached to a wooden base.

Carding: using carders to tease and open wool out to separate the individual fibres.

Combed tops: commercially prepared fibres, combed into long loose ropes. Fibres in the rope are parallel, well separated and ideal for making lightweight felt.

Felt: a fabric in which wool fibres are interlocked and entangled. With the application of moisture and friction, they are transformed into a compact mass and become felt.

Fibre: for felting purposes, individual strands of wool, grown collectively as fleece on a sheep. Other animals produce hair fibres. Fibres can also be of vegetable origin (for example, cotton) or synthetic (for example, polyester).

Fleece: unprocessed wool shorn from a sheep.

Inlay: technique in felt design in which pre-felted pieces are placed on a background batt of unfelted fibres and the whole is then felted together.

Loom-state cotton muslin: unwashed, soft cotton muslin, straight from the loom with none of the usual fillers which are added during the finishing processes of cloth.

Merino: a breed of sheep producing fine wool of 60s count upwards. Merino sheep are of Spanish origin, but thrive in Australia, New Zealand and South Africa.

Micron: a measurement of fibre thickness: one millionth of a metre. Microns are used as an alternative to the Bradford Count. The lower the number, the finer the fibre.

Milling: a process to increase the density of felt by compacting it with extra heat and friction, used on heavy and sturdy felts.

Mosaic: a design built up of felted pieces slotted into each other, placed on background felt and the whole quilted together.

Needle felt: fine batts of carded fibres pass under a bed of barbed felting needles. As needles pass through fibres, the lower layers are pulled up through the top layers. The continuous process produces a sheet of wool fibres which may then be wet-felted.

Nuno: wool fibres forming a design and felted on to fabric. As the wool shrinks, it pulls the fabric with it and produces interesting gathered areas.

Pre-felt: the fibres are cross-layered and felted just enough to form a cohesive sheet, but have not begun to shrink.

Resist: a plastic template used in making hollow felted forms to prevent layers of fibres felting together. Also, a binding used in shibori dyeing techniques.

Rovings: long, thin ropes of fibres produced towards the end of the commercial process of spinning wool yarns. Much finer than wool tops; similar to a single wool yarn with no twist.

Scales: the distinctive feature of animal fibres which make the fibre rough in one direction and smooth in the other. Scales are the essential characteristic that enables wool to felt.

Shibori: a Japanese technique for shaping and patterning fabric.

Sliver: a fine strip of carded fibres, pulled out into a long fine length.

Throwing: a process in making nuno felt. The bundle of felt is repeatedly dropped gently and the resulting vibrations encourage the fibre to shrink.

Bibliography

Right: Little Fishes *(Sarah Lawrence)*. *One of a series based on fish motifs. Decorative handmade felt embroidered, gilded and embellished with beads.*

Burkett, M E. *The Art of the Feltmaker*. Abbot Hall Art Gallery, Kendal, 1979

Paetau Sjöberg, Gunilla. *Felt: new directions for an ancient craft*. Interweave Press, 1996

Smith, Sheila and Walker, Freda. *Felt-making: the Whys and Wherefores*. Dalefelt Publications, 1995, reprinted 2005

Wada, Yoshiko. *Memory on Cloth: Shibori Now*. Kodansha International, 2002.

Useful Addresses and Suppliers

USEFUL ADDRESSES

For further information on all aspects of felt and felt-making, contact *The International Feltmakers Association*. **www.feltmakers.com**

For further information on sheep breeds, contact *The British Wool Marketing Board*. **www.britishwool.org.uk**

SUPPLIERS

Fibres

craftynotions.com
Unit 2, Jessop Way
Newark
NG24 2ER
01636 659 890
www.craftynotions.com

Fibrecrafts
Old Portsmouth Road
Peasmarsh
Guildford
Surrey GU3 1LZ
01483 565 800
www.fibrecrafts.com

Handweavers Studio & Gallery Ltd
29 Haroldstone Road
London E17 7AN
020 8521 2281
www.handweaversstudio.co.uk

Wingham Wool Work
70 Main Street
Wentworth
Rotherham
South Yorkshire S62 7TN
01226 742 926

Adelaide Walker
Bays 55/56 Pegholme
Wharfebank Business Centre
Otley Mills, Ilkley Road
Otley, West Yorkshire LS21 3JP
01943 850 812

Fabrics

Whaleys (Bradford) Ltd
Harris Court
Great Horton Road
Bradford BD7 4EQ
01274 576718
www.whaleys-bradford.ltd.uk

Silk fabrics/fabric paints/embroidery threads

Rainbow Silks
85 High Street
Great Missenden
Bucks HP16 0AL
01494 862 111
www.rainbowsilks.co.uk

Fabric paints and dyes

Art Van Go
The Studios
1 Stevenage Road
Knebworth
Hertfordshire
SG3 6AN
01438 814 946
www.artvango.co.uk

Gaywool Dyes
The Threshing Barn
Lower Lady Meadows Farm
Nr Bradnop
Leek
Staffordshire ST13 7EZ
www.threshingbarn.com

Kemtex Colours
Chorley Business & Technology Centre
Euxton Lane
Chorley
Lancashire PR7 6TE
01257 230 220
www.kemtex.co.uk

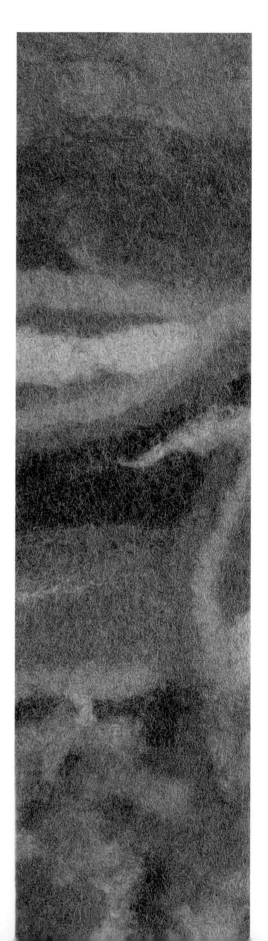

Index